GOD MADE MAN

DISCOVERING YOUR PURPOSE AND LIVING AN INTENTIONAL LIFE

DR. SCOTT SILVERII

 Five
Stones
Press

CONTENTS

All Scripture quotations, unless otherwise indicated, are taken from the New American Standard Bible, ©1960, 1962, 1963, 1968, 1971, 1972, 1973, 1975, 1977, 1995 by The Lockman Foundation. Used by permission.

Other versions used are:

KJV—King James Version. Authorized King James Version.

NIV—Scripture taken from the Holy Bible, New International Version®. Copyright © 1973, 1978, 1984 by International Bible Society. Used by permission of Zondervan Publishing House. All rights reserved.

First Edition

Cover Design: Wicked Smart Designs

Editorial Team: Imogen Howsen

Interior Formatting: Five Stones Press Design Team

Publisher: Five Stones Press, Dallas, Texas

For quantity sales, textbooks, and orders by trade bookstores or wholesalers contact Five Stones Press at publish@fivestonespress.net

Five Stones Press is owned and operated by Five Stones Church, a nonprofit 501c3 religious organization. Press name and logo are trademarked. Contact publisher for use.

Dr. Scott Silverii's website is scottsilverii.com

Printed in the United States of America

This book is for you.
You may or may not know this, but you were created for something
incredible. Just the fact that your heart beats inside your chest, and life's
blood pumps through your veins is a miracle of creation. From that point on,
how incredible you become is up to you.

THE MAN IN THE ARENA

"It is not the critic who counts; not the man who points out how the strong man stumbles, or where the doer of deeds could have done them better. The credit belongs to the man who is actually in the arena, whose face is marred by dust and sweat and blood; who strives valiantly; who errs, who comes short again and again, because there is no effort without error and shortcoming; but who does actually strive to do the deeds; who knows great enthusiasms, the great devotions; who spends himself in a worthy cause; who at the best knows in the end the triumph of high achievement, and who at the worst, if he fails, at least fails while daring greatly, so that his place shall never be with those cold and timid souls who neither know victory nor defeat."

Theodore Roosevelt, April 23, 1910

INTRODUCTION

"I'm leaving."

It was the final straw in what had been a horrible year since I retired as a chief of police in another state and relocated to Dallas with my family.

Slamming the door behind me, I marched into the cold, driving rain. Juggling the keys in my palm, I still wasn't sure where it was I was going, or why. But I'd had enough.

Retirement was supposed to be an incredible, carefree adventure. Leah and I would do all of the things we wanted to do and go places we wanted to see. Easy life, right?

I slipped as I ran through the rain to get into my Jeep. I also failed to avoid the smash of rainwater that dashed over the lip of the canvas top and dumped across my shirt's sleeve. I didn't care anymore. I just wanted out.

Soon, I became twisted in the madness of what is known as Dallas traffic. I desperately peered through sheets of water washing over my windshield, and finally threw the phone to the floorboard because I couldn't get service to strike up the GPS. I thought I knew where the medical clinic was located, so if I could only get within striking distance, I could figure out the rest. Sure, Leah and I had argued about me going there, but after a year of stress, deep depression, weight gain and loneliness, I was desperate for help and wasn't sure where else to look.

For some crazy reason, I was trying to find a weight loss clinic. I'd ballooned up to 270 pounds, my blood pressure was rocketing so high my eyes actually throbbed, and all I wanted to do was sleep. Shoving me deeper into darkness was the reality that only a year prior, I had been "The Man" back in my south Louisiana city. I was a well-known chief of police, a college professor and an expert national speaker on everything from data-driven policing to mystery writing.

As I frantically watched for street signs and avoiding rear bumpers, I was lost in a city where no one knew my name, offered no free passes because I once wore a badge, or recognized me as "Chief." It wasn't until two hours later that I skulked back home. Truthfully, I was so lost that I'd never traveled more than four miles from where I'd started. I was lost, alone, and worst of all; I was no longer The Man.

Standing in the driving rain outside of our home's darkened front door, I tugged my sopping wet shirt over the paddle holster in my waistband. My elbow tapped against the pistol's grip out of weapon retention habit. It would've been so easy to be done with it right then and there. The kids weren't home and Leah knew I'd been struggling over a final solution. I hesitated because I knew there were only two choices left for me in this life. Let me tell you about the one I chose.

Armor Up,
Scott

1

INTENTIONALLY DISCOVERING YOUR PURPOSE

I'd like to start this off with a promise. I'm not going to bore you with another feel-good, pat-on-the-back book that gets tossed onto your wife's nightstand. I don't read them either. This is a conversation between you and me.

I wrote this in hopes of encouraging you to embrace your alpha manhood without having to worry about being attacked for it. Now, the truth is, we can do better. In some cases, much better, but until we know where we've been, there's no way we'll ever know where we're going.

Can we continue to crawl through the same daily grind? Sure, and we might just reach the grand old age of average life expectancy. But would you rather steal home base with a scorching headfirst dive while avoiding an All-Star catcher, or stroll across the plate because the pitcher walked a batter on loaded bases?

Honestly, if the latter is your choice, this might not be for you. Nah, I'm kidding, but what does matter is that we round the bases and finish this gift called life stronger than we began. I say life is a gift because that's a theme you'll see throughout this power hitter. God gave us this life, and it is a precious gift, and no matter what society, your family or even your friends may say, you are an amazing gift because God created you to be so.

I know most of us have treated our gift as if it were a little brother's birthday present, but when you think back to all of the stupid stuff we did, and how lucky we are to be alive, it really is amazing to be here at all. So, since we're here at this moment together, how about we give this a look and see what's going on about this business of manhood.

Man As Man

There's so much static these days about men, but I'm going to cut through the fog and not worry about being PC (politically correct) or stepping on toes. I can apologize later if that's what it takes to keep you in the game, but for now, let's set some ground rules for getting through the book. The purpose is to encourage you to build the better man. Not that you aren't freaking incredible the way you are, but let's be honest, if there weren't at least a few rough edges in your life, you wouldn't be reading this.

And, if God Made Man was given to you by someone as a "gift," then maybe you haven't noticed how rough your patches are. As for me, I'm still sanding down rough spots, and working to be that better man, so there's zero judgment. This is more like teamwork than telling you what to do. We men are stronger together anyways, right?

> And if one prevail against him, two shall withstand him;
>   and a threefold cord is not quickly broken.
> Ecclesiastes 4:12

The scope is simple. How do we go about moving from where we are to where we know we were meant to be? No one's life has been perfect up to this point and pretending it has been isn't going to help you move the better-life needle one inch. I'm not asking for a show of hands but being honest with yourself while reading this is going to go a long way toward helping you become more purposeful and intentional in your path toward being a better man.

Before we start twisting wrenches and sparking up the torch out in the man cave, I want to throw another truth at you. I like to offer men what I call "bailouts." Those are opportunities when you're really not digging a tough situation, so you get to exit without feeling bad about being at the right place for the wrong reason.

It's like getting up and going to the bathroom in church. It's awkward, so you just hold on, but you're miserable. Now, if they offered a bailout by turning off the lights or something, then there'd be an exodus to the potty like kindergarteners after lunch.

The bailouts I'll offer along the way of this book are when I know we're approaching a crossroads that'll require making a decision one way or the other. I'm not saying there aren't other options for becoming the God made man, but I'm going to stick to the blueprint written by the Creator.

And let's be honest, not every man is going to want to improve by drawing into a posture reflecting God. Some men are happy to wake up and see that there's not a police chalk line drawn around their body. They figure that they've lucked out another day, so why not get up, take their chances and see what happens while they're awake.

There is so much more to life than merely crawling by. We were created to be rulers, conquerors, kings and priests. It's in God's holy Word. Oh, by the way, everything I'm going to share with you is based on His Word. After all, who would you rather trust for ageless, sage advice: me or the big guy? But, in the event that you didn't see the writing on the wall, you could bail out now if you're totally averse to my leaning on God's Word to hang out with you.

Still here? Awesome, and God bless you. Building the better man is certainly subjective as to the condition of "better," so we're going to focus on the spirit-man as much as the natural-man. While the earthly definitions are varied, there's a pretty consistent standard for living life as a God-made man. Setting our face toward God allows us to know His ultimate goal for why He created us in the first place. This in turn will help us chart our own paths toward an incredible life of victory. I like this brief and to the point verse from Colossians 3:2:

Set your minds on things above, not on earthly things.

Truth and Consequences

Ever wonder why this was all created in the first place? When I began thinking bigger and allowing my mind to roam beyond yesterday's sports scores, it soon became uncomfortable, so I stopped. I limited myself and my awareness to just what was within my grasp. Like whatever is on the middle shelf in your fridge: it's easy, so we go for it. But we miss out on the opportunity to have enjoyed something much better with only a little effort to look past the expired milk.

I recall many decades ago while in college, sitting on a porch step with my girlfriend at the time. I was in my freshman year minoring in psychology, so I assumed I had a depth of universal knowledge that would immediately impress her. Actually, I just figured I'd blow her mind with my nineteen-year-old wisdom gained from sandlot football and Saturday morning cartoons.

The truth is, as we stared up into an endless, star-speckled opportunity to understand what it was we were mindlessly looking at or looking for, I had zero idea what I was saying. I wasn't even sure if she was listening, but it really didn't matter until she asked the one question that every deep-thinking Bro has pondered. No, not that.

She asked, "What's the meaning of it all?"

I catalogued my best 1980s MTV music lyrics (yes, this was in the early 80's) and my mind drew a blank. I was going to recite a line or two from someone like John Cougar Mellencamp or Cyndi Lauper. But the bigness of her question and the smallness of my testosterone-driven mind caused me to waffle within the potential for delivering a life-changing response.

"Love," I finally whispered.

She smiled and I saw the twinkle in her eye. Yes, she agreed that it was indeed all about love. I exhaled off to the side because I knew I'd just dodged a bullet and had also potentially made a little headway with her. And just like that, her dad walked out onto the porch and said those fateful words that I'll never forget.

"Go home, Scott. You're drunk."

You know the worst part about that night so long ago, besides being immediately humiliated after delivering such an amazing pickup line to an incredible-looking girl? Her dad was right. I was drunk, and I was extremely shallow in my emotional understanding of anything beyond having a good time at everyone else's expense. So why share that swing and miss?

When I began writing God Made Man, I started out with a first draft, and then many more to follow until someone finally said I had to stop rewriting the opening sentence over and over again. But in those early attempts I was going to roll out my resume on a regal red carpet and allow you the time to be royally impressed. Not that I was expecting you to applaud loudly and call out my name as you set a personal record in your latest CrossFit competition, but I wouldn't stop you if you had chosen to do so.

Instead of doing what we men do best by showing the world a mask of what we've accomplished, I decided to share with you the truth of who I am. Well, in that example it was a glimpse of who I was. In this book I knew it was best to begin with the very same thing we'll end with, and that is the truth. I think men connect best when we stop measuring macho resumes and amazing feats of audacity, and instead accept each other as we are. I wanted to share the truth about my life in hopes you'll find connection points that help you to say, "You too?"

Yes, me too, and so many other men who want to do better but might not know how to do better. Within the layers of what makes us who we are, there is a physical body, a soul and a spirit. Most of my life I abused my body, numbed my soul and denied my spirit. Sure, I tried to cover up what was empty inside with a laundry list of accomplishments, but in the end, just like on the porch that fateful summer night, I had nothing inside.

Once we commit to dropping the tattered bags holding our busted trophies and dog-eared certificates, and seek God's purpose, then we'll understand His desire for our lives. It all starts with Him, and in this truth, I'll share why we are here. You see, although I was young, dumb and full of Keystone Light at the time, I was actually right when I slurred out the word, "Love."

Of course, her dad knew that the love I was talking about had nothing to do with Jesus and everything to do with the daughter he wasn't going to lose to some poacher passed out on his front porch.

It was in love that we were created for relationship. God created us to glorify Him, and that's why we were made in His image. We are not some single-cell organism that belly-crawled from prehistoric goo (bailout alert on anti-evolutionism) to evolve over millions of years into the studs we are today. God created us to be perfect like Him, and He did it out of love.

Check out Genesis 1:26 where God the Father is talking with Jesus the Son and the Holy Spirit about you and me.

Then God said, "Let us make mankind in our image, in our likeness, so that they may rule over the fish in the sea and the birds in the sky, over the livestock and all the wild animals, and over all the creatures that move along the ground."

I underlined a few cool points in this very important scripture. I'm not going to assume you do or don't dig into the Bible. Honestly, the men who get so wrapped up in their own religious interpretation of what God is trying to lay out are the ones I avoid. But I do want to keep it straight and accurate for the sake of laying down this foundational principle to better man building.

You are not an accident. You were purposefully created by an intentional act of God. When He says, "let us" and "in our," He is talking about the Trinity, which is God the Father, Christ the Son and the Holy Spirit. Remember earlier when I said we were intended to be rulers, conquerors, kings and priests? Here is the very first mention of what we were placed on this earth to do—*"that they rule over..."*

That scripture is powerful truth. There is no way of getting around it or denying it. So, if you're still on the fence about evolution of the species, then it's an argument you'll have to take up with God. Otherwise, it's pretty clear, my brother ruler of everything, that we were intentionally created in God's image for a very special purpose.

Now you may be asking, "But what happened?"

Consequences are what happened. There are consequences for sin, and one of the most serious is described in Romans 6 and is death.

> For the wages of sin is death, but the gift of God is
> eternal life in Christ Jesus our Lord.
> Romans 6:23

Although physical death is surely a possibility, the death referenced in Romans is exactly the death experienced by Adam and Eve when they sinned in the garden of Eden. Death is separation from God. You see, when we sin, there are consequences. In those unconfessed consequences, we are doomed to scraping through a life alone and absent of God. Now you might say that's no big deal but compare the blessed life of favor enjoyed by Adam in the garden to the life of hardship he suffered once exiled because of sin.

So how did we go from being God's right-hand man to getting kicked out and spawning generations of broken brothers? It was sin and its consequence of death. Of course, God made sure there was a better door to open before closing Adam's. In that second door is what the Bible refers to as the Second Adam. Not another failed natural-man, but a glorious victor in the spirit-man of Jesus Christ.

Looking at this from another angle, "bearing fruit" is a cool expression through the Bible, and one that you should take time to meditate over. It starts with sowing and reaping. Let's say you eat junk food (sowing), then what you will get is fat (reaping). Same thing in the construction process of building the better man. If you cut corners, cheat and look for the easy way out, you'll suffer the consequences and won't have the personal foundation to sustain success.

Alternatively, choosing to believe in God and purposefully avoiding sin by the daily decisions you make will prosper you in His kingdom. Now don't misunderstand the word prosper as in prosperity gospel or the get rich with Jesus false teachings. Prosperity comes in many forms but those such as health, peace, love and joy are so much more vital than cash in your pocket.

Wow that was a crazy long, run-on sentence. Point is, there is no straddling the fence with faith. Either you are all in on your belief that God is real, or you aren't. There is no neutral ground. I know you're invested in living the blessed life. Great call!

God doesn't lie, tease, give false hope or waste eternal efforts trying to jerk you around. What He says, He means. If it doesn't become real, it's because of your jacked-up process of sowing and reaping.

Read this promise and tell me what you think God is saying to you. I'm serious about this; take your time. Break it down. Allow it to speak to you. Proclaim the promises. Willingly accept God's blessings. This is power packed, so please absorb every word. This is your life after all, and I want you to live it like the alpha male God created you to be!

> I am the vine; you are the branches. If you remain in me
> and I in you, you will bear much fruit; apart from me
> you can do nothing. If you do not remain in me, you
> are like a branch that is thrown away and withers;
> such branches are picked up, thrown into the fire and
> burned. If you remain in me and my words remain in
> you, ask whatever you wish, and it will be done for
> you. This is to my Father's glory, that you bear much
> fruit, showing yourselves to be my disciples.
> John 15:5-8

You see, I may have suffered the consequences of being a slobbering drunk muscle-head in college, but God allowed me a second chance through the spirit-man as reflected in Christ. And when I proudly guessed at the word love for my soon-to-be-never-seen-again, I was unwittingly correct. It is all about love. It's about God's love for us and not only that He created us, but also why He created us.

Why Are We Here?

Have you ever taken the time to ask what's it all about? Between the hustle of life and the bustle of trying to make your way within its stream, there are times when we question our purpose. I'd imagine the answer is like mine in that we've got way too much stuff to do to sit around worrying about the why.

The irony is that the core of the question, "why?" is simple, yet it's either avoided or misunderstood. God created us with a purpose... That purpose is to glorify Him. Now, I can see where some might take this to mean that God was selfish because He created for himself His own little cheerleading squad: "Go God!!!"

> ...everyone who is called by my name, whom I
> created for my glory, whom I formed and made.
> Isaiah 43:7

The truth is that God did not need us. He doesn't have an ego to pump or people to high-five. When you look back over the course of human history, we've pretty much made a mess of things. So, when the Bible says to glorify Him, it is only out of His love that we were created, and for love that we remain. We were created out of God, so in us is a piece of Him. Because He is love, then we too are a reflection of that love.

Did that paragraph about love make you want to grab the man card out of my hand and thrash it into a heap of scraps? I can understand that, because I would've wanted to do the same thing at one point in my life. What changed? I learned that I didn't have to be so hard in my life to be tough. I was a man who never showed emotion, and I never cut myself slack in anything—ever. When I came to understand what it was to build the better man, I realized that the capacity to give and receive love was the key.

I'm going to pound on my chest for a bit. I might not have known it back then, and her dad sure didn't appreciate me when I said it, but love was the right answer after all. Too bad I was too blind to see the truth, although I did suffer the consequences.

2

WHAT IS THE GOD MADE MAN?

Laying the foundation to build the better man begins with accepting Jesus Christ into your life as Lord and Savior. What does that look like, you might ask, and will it mean I don't get to have fun any longer? On the surface these might seem like odd questions, but I promise these are conversations I've had with other men over the years.

Don't let religion get in the way. It's unfortunate that once we feel the tug for Christ we get discouraged by rules and rituals of whatever church we happen to walk into. Don't confuse faith with religion. Too many religions turn people away from God because their focus is on what else? Joining their religion.

Accepting Christ into your life is between you and Jesus. The keys are that you want to know Him, and you accept that you are a sinner. This isn't to beat yourself up, but it's to understand that you've lived a life apart from God, and in that separation you have sinned.

You are asking God to forgive you, and He will. You don't have to pay anything, do anything or know anybody. God's grace of salvation is a free gift to you because His Son, Jesus, paid the ultimate price.

You can do this in your car, in your house or on your jog around the lake. It doesn't matter where you are or when you do it. What matters is that you pray about it and ask God to come into your life. Why doesn't Jesus just come on in if He knows you're hurting or need Him?

Great question. Free will. God allows us the freedom to choose Him or not choose Him. It's your choice, or otherwise how could you love Him if you were forced to do so? Jesus is standing at the door and waiting for you to allow Him in, but He won't kick in that door like the point man on a SWAT team.

> Behold, I stand at the door, and knock: if any man hear
> my voice, and open the door, I will come in to him,
> and will sup with him, and he with me.
> Revelation 3:20

So now that you've asked Christ into your life, it's time to learn more about Him. It's like accepting a roommate into your condo. Y'all are going to be living together and hanging out, so wouldn't you want to know everything about Him? Christ is that way, and the more you get to know Him, the more you'll want to be just like Him.

How can I be so sure? Because the more you know Jesus, the more you know yourself. Christ is not some stranger who wants to mind control you. He is you: the very best of you. It's that desire to know Him that will guide your power to grow in Him.

Oh, and you asked about whether or not being a Christian allowed you to have fun anymore. I guess that depends on your definition of fun. If what you call fun has led to drama, addiction, abandonment, failures in life and a general feeling that life stinks, then I imagine you'd be eager to escape that "fun."

Now, imagine living life with peace, true happiness, no drama, blessings beyond your imagination, and an assurance that God the Father will always be there to watch your six as well as lead your way. I can assure you there will be more fulfillment in your life with Christ than you've ever known in the nightclubs, the gym or happy hour out by the pool.

Being Purposeful

We've got to purposefully go about building the better man. I'm not saying you can't do it on your own, but since it's just us and we agreed to shoot straight, think about where you are in life. Are you satisfied? If so, amen. But do you honestly believe that you are living life as full and blessed as God wants for you?

Or maybe you're thinking why can't we just draw a line in the sand and promise to do good from that point forward? Because we were born into the bloodline of the original sin of man (Adam and Eve), and we all carry a lifetime of experiences that influence our way forward.

Some good and some not so good. It's the not-so-goods that refuse to remain dormant. Trust me, they will rear their hurtful heads at some point in the course of your life. Without the solid foundation of having become the better man, you chance collapsing.

Pursuing God's will is what begins separating us from the past of pain, failure and sin that once defined us. We don't have the capacity in our natural-man to just stop patterns that have become engrained throughout our life. Change comes first from the spirit-man because as God promises, we are new creations in Christ.

Part of becoming new is gaining the heart to submit to His will. Submission is not weakness. It takes a strong man of conviction to say they will purposefully give authority of their life over to God. It's an ultimate act of courage and love.

Think about Navy SEALs for a moment. Do you see them as weak? Consider that individually each are incredibly strong men, but to have become a SEAL, and to remain a SEAL, they made a choice to surrender. They chose to surrender to an authority they trusted to break off the unhealthy pieces of their pasts and rebuild them with the tools to become ultimate warriors. Still think surrendering is weakness. Me neither.

> Therefore, if anyone is in Christ, the new creation has
> come: The old has gone, the new is here!
> 2 Corinthians 5:17

Brother, if you hold onto anything I've shared so far, please let it be this promise from God Himself. I know you know He's real. Otherwise you would've cut bait a few sections earlier. This is straight from Him, and it is truth. Once you accept Christ into your life, you are made new.

What is it that has gone away? Is it depression, thoughts of suicide, shame from sexual abuse, divorce, adultery, failing as a dad to your kids, as a husband, sexual sin, addiction, porn, gambling, pain from your past, fear of the future, and on and on and on...

This is your time to smash free from what it is that has held you hostage from living a blessed life. God didn't create the drama in life, sin did. You've been washed clean. Whether you dumpster-dive back into the muck is up to you.

What are you going to choose?

Your Choice

This isn't one of those late-night infomercials or an *act now* ad on social media. Making the choice to build the better man is an intentional decision that will require your full attention. It's not going to happen because you bought this book and it's not going to happen because you walked into church one day. It's a choice, and an action, and a commitment to continue that action, and an acceptance that your choice to act is going to build the better man.

I wish it were as easy as taking a pill. If that were the case, count me in, but the truth is, we're not just going to be able to snap our fingers and expect it to have been done. I'll share this story from my past because it's another example of how stupid I was, and also how life's lessons can lead to revelations about making the right choices for our life.

I powerlifted back in my college days. I should've been studying, but no one ever got attention from holding a shaky C average in freshman remedial courses, so I focused on what did—being big and strong. I thought my mind was holding me back because when I saw the plates stacked on the bench press bar, I'd start doubting because it was heavier than I'd ever done before. I had a great idea. I'd trust the other knuckleheads I trained with to out-psych my psyche.

I placed a blindfold over my eyes, laid down on the solid bench, and told my gym partners to put on whatever amount of weight they thought I could press. I made the choice to set my mind free from my past experiences and allow my potential to smash a new personal record. It was go time.

"Okay, Moose," they said.

Yes, that was also a clue about my past. My college nickname was Moose.

I could hear the steel plates rattling as the guys grunted to hoist the barbell off of the rack. Once my arms were locked out up top, and my chest full of air, I said, "Okay."

Five hundred pounds of steel came crashing down onto my frame as both arms collapsed beneath the weight and my ego. What did I learn? It wasn't their place to make decisions about my potential. I was ignorant to place my life, safety and future blindly in the hands of others who were not completely invested in me. And finally, that I couldn't bench press five hundred pounds. Of course, that lesson came immediately, but what I knew was that building anything from muscle to manhood requires a purposeful effort.

What Is Better?

I always have to bite my tongue when someone asks a question and the reply is, "It depends." I want a clear, concise and definitive answer. But then I understand that there is no "one" answer when dealing with much else beyond math. Unless you were me, and there was no telling what an equation's reply might look like.

The nuts and bolts of God Made Man is that I want to give you the tools to build a foundation that will support and sustain your better man. If you want a closer walk with Christ, then that's going to look a lot different from a man who is struggling to free himself from the shackles of porn. And, while fighting to break free from the pain of your past, the foundations are the same as battling depression and thoughts of suicide.

Although we agree on not liking the "it depends" reply, it really is very different for each one of us, and yet still very much the same. That's the beauty of this book being based upon God's Word. See, He doesn't shift gears when things get hot. His Word is the same yesterday, today and forever. If and when you get to a point of struggling over your progress, and you're questioning the validity of this series, please know that these words are timeless, tested and true.

3

BUT WHO ARE YOU?

I've got a novel idea.

Most do-it-better books start off with the author's story. They usually share a testimony that is so incredibly tragic or so blessed that we get lost in the spread of circumstances. I'm just going to run this right down the middle. Most, if not all, of us have had bad times that defined or shaped us, so I'm not sharing my experiences to compete with you. I'll only do it to relate with you.

I grew up completely godless. Not until I moved away for college did I begin to understand the whole God, Jesus and the Holy Spirit situation. Of course, I went to college in Mississippi's Bible belt so there wasn't much choice. I'll backtrack a bit, or otherwise it'll make for a historically short chapter, and you'll be on your way to the dumpster with this book.

We never stepped foot in church as a family. I don't recall going there for Christmas or the *make everyone dress up with plaid bowties and short pants* Easter outing. I mean, nothing. We weren't heathens, it just wasn't a priority for my folks, so we all suffered as a result.

Even in the vacuum of faith, I always felt the tug of God in my heart. But because He was a stranger, it was uncomfortable and even scary as a kid to feel "something" was out there. But what? Did you know your first impression of God comes from your folks, and mostly your dad? If your dad was absent or scarce, then you may have found your God example in a grandfather, uncle, coach, pastor or teacher. If there was no one, you may still be searching for who and what God is to you.

Thanks to a dysfunctional relationship with a dominant dad, I thought of my heavenly Father as cold, silent, domineering and always waiting to smack me when I screwed up. Eventually, I learned that the best way to avoid getting hurt by either was to avoid both of them. Besides, how could my dad or my God love me when neither "father" cared enough to stop me from making so many stupid mistakes that caused such extreme pain?

I'd be willing to bet that most of us grew up with a dominant parent in the house. Now I'd bet that many of us grew to become dominant in some way or another. There's no judgment because we #1 – do what we see, and #2 – often confuse being in charge with what is actually domineering. It suppresses the spirit and crushes the souls of those beneath the weight of oppression.

My dad dominated our family with silence. No one was allowed to express how they felt, or even when they hurt physically or emotionally. It was silence, or it was discipline. I think the question I was asked more than anything else was, "You wanna backhand?" I mean seriously, how do you answer that as a child?

Because there was no interest in what I did, I was free to do as I wanted as long as I avoided my dad's belt. So there I was in my white tube socks with stripes and numbers on the side. I also had my high school football undershirt that rested somewhere between my belly button and nipples, and my case of occasional teenaged acne.

What could go wrong, right? Well, other than being an eleven-year-old who taught himself to drive after midnight in strangers' cars, and becoming a weeknight barroom regular at fifteen, recklessness became the pattern of my broken life.

No matter how mature we might've thought we were as kids, living a grown-up life and doing destructive grown-up things was never designed to bear fruit. Although I didn't understand it at the time, I was desperate for attention. Actually, I was getting plenty of attention—negative.

What I needed wasn't more discipline because I'd grown numb to the hurt. It was my parents' mentoring and affection that I was so desperate for. What I really needed throughout my entire life was to know that someone actually gave a crap about me.

It wasn't found at home, so I began to seek it elsewhere. The place I found attention was through physical sex. There's no way that, as a twelve-year-old boy, I was equipped to handle what sex would do to my mind and body. But, despite the chaos, sex became the only thing that made me not hate myself so much.

It gave me moments of feeling wanted, but just like any destructive cycle, the lows got much deeper than the highs of sex could ever deliver. I'd become addicted, and sex caused destruction throughout my life. Yeah, even after I was married.

Most of us who struggle with addictions or overcompensate are usually tirelessly trying to fill a void created long ago by the lack of what we all basically desire—human relationship.

In September 2016, I sat at my dad's deathbed over several days as he slipped into and out of consciousness. I openly prayed for him and spoke words of peace as his hours drew limited. I was blessed to have him lucid three times over those days. I knew in his final moments on earth that he'd make amends for those he hurt. I was so anxious to hear him say, "I love you." After all, it was only three words that I'd needed to hear my entire life.

With his last breath, he took those words with him to the grave.

I'll tell you the truth: it hurt and it still does, but I did as God my Father told me to do. I forgave him. Not only did I forgive him, but I honored him. Honor your parents by forgiving them. God commands that we honor our parents. Specifically, He says:

> Honor your father and your mother: that your days may
>   be long on the land which the Lord your God
>   gives you.
> Exodus 20:12

Nowhere does this say to judge your dad, ignore him because you don't approve of his decisions, or hold anything he did or didn't do to you against him. This simply says to honor him. The reward for your willingness to do so is a fulfilled life. Honor comes in various forms, so you decide which method is best for you, but before you can bless your parents with honor, you must forgive.

The Other Intro

Had I begun this section with my professional resume like I mentioned earlier, you would've called BS as the book sailed out the window. But don't litter, it's the only planet we have!! The truth is, I was also addicted to consumption of worldly accolades. It's like we keep bumping into the same issues, but it's because we have that basic need for relationship.

In the beginning; yes, the very beginning, God provided for love, security and significance in the relationship with Adam. They are three of our most basic desires. When we walk apart from Him, we're left to find those on our own. I sought love through sexual relationships, security in my own alpha tough-guy occupation, and significance through my degrees, trophies, and social acceptance.

What I'd mistaken as career drive and personal pursuits of achievement, were in reality more of the same ways of trying to dull my pain. Medicating my personal injuries had become the only way I found reasons to continue from one day to the next.

This obsession racked up numerous titles, diplomas and accolades. I lived an exciting and dangerous life, and was promoted in part because of my endless enthusiasm for doing the job no matter what it required me to do. I also earned a master's degree and a PhD while working to feed my full-time obsession that was satiating my full-time pain.

Most importantly, I was the man who fixed problems, saved the day and faced the most violent of criminals when they threatened the peace. I was a fixer and doer extraordinaire. These were the things welded to my identity. I couldn't release them any more than I would've been able to take the heart out of my chest. Being in charge was who I was and what I did. Yet, never was I more empty than when surrounded by others and my "trophies."

Guess what? Nothing I've ever desired, made or won lasted. But, God's love endures forever.

What is your identity attached to? Has God tugged on certain areas of your life, but you tugged back? Are you more focused on being The Man than on being God's son? Let's take a peek at exactly what it looks like to be God's son, and the man He called to serve His kingdom by following Him and leading your household.

It may look a lot different from how you imagined.

God graciously gifted me with another chance. He was generous in allowing me to marry, and fulfill a role I had failed at before: being a husband and a father. He has given me a path and the partner for removing the layers of guilt so my injuries would finally heal. And He has graciously showed me that He not only loves me, but has wonderful plans for my service to Him.

What has God done for you? Has He helped you to see where your pain began? Are you moving your injuries into His healing light? Has He shown you His plans for your life's service to Him?

These are a few serious questions to ask yourself. I know this chapter was supposed to be about me, but truth be told, this entire book is about you. I'm just here to prayerfully help you get to you.

4

MAN UP ACTION ITEMS

I'm sincerely thankful you've come this far. I know the content has been tough at times, and it's easy to turn away when the mirror's reflection isn't as positive as we want it to be. It doesn't mean we're bad, it just means there's work to do.

The most important thing we need to do at this stage in our life is to Man Up. When you see that term what does it bring to mind? I know for me it has meant different things at different times in my life. When sexual temptation ruled my life, it meant time to make the move for sex. When I loved the violence of a good barroom brawl, it meant keeping my fists up and my chin down.

When there was a dangerous undercover operation, it meant keeping my team alert so I could make the deal and come out safe. When I wanted to graduate with my PhD, it meant setting priorities and getting the studies done. When my wife was going to leave me because of infidelity, it meant confessing, repenting and regaining her trust moment by moment.

What does Man Up mean to you?

To Man Up the God way also means many things depending on what season of life you are in. The verse that speaks to me about what it is to be a Godly man is found here in the New King James Version:

Watch, stand fast in the faith, be brave, be strong. Let
all that you do be done with love.
1 Corinthians 16:13-14

This tells us to keep watch and be the protector that alpha men were created to be. Remember that God placed Adam in the garden to watch over and protect His creations. Next, men are to stand fast in the faith. This is our trust in Jesus no matter how hard life gets or how tempted we may be to go back to the old ways. God's Word then encourages us to be brave. I love the way Nelson Mandela expresses it.

"I learned that courage was not the absence of fear, but
the triumph over it. The brave man is not he who
does not feel afraid, but he who conquers that fear."

—*Nelson Mandela*

God continues by instructing us to be strong. Most men also like hearing this. But strength is just like the term Man Up, it means so many different things based upon the season of your life. Strong can mean remaining married when times get tough, handing your life over to Jesus when you'd rather take control and work it out alone, or finding strength through surrender and service to others.

The most beautiful part of these instructions on manhood is that in everything we do, we do it in love. These two sentences give us our marching orders better than anything I've ever seen. God isn't against the alpha male. God is THE Alpha and the Omega. God just wants us to follow His guide for what an alpha man is supposed to be. Watchful, faithful, brave, strong and loving. When you think about it, how perfectly simple is God's plan for men?

These qualities create the ultimate framework for being an intentional man of God. It's also important we understand how to place these ideals into action. I mean, how cool would it be to hang out being watchful, faithful, brave, strong and loving? But where's the action in the alpha lifestyle?

While there are unlimited words we could use to paint a picture of what a Godly man might look like, I've prayed over these qualities and know they're meant to not only describe God's character, but also appeal to what an alpha male most appreciates.

Man of Action Item 1:

The first man of action item I see as important in living as a Godly man is being willing to repent when we sin. Trust me, you will sin even after accepting Christ as your Savior and being forgiven of your sins. There is a process of pursuing God's forgiveness throughout our trials and stumbles. When we fall, God is there to give us a hand up, but we've still got to be willing to reach out.

We'll also sin or offend others along our journey. I was so stubborn and can hardly recall uttering the words "I'm sorry" through most of my life. It wasn't until I began to live the spiritual alpha male life that I was able to stop causing hurt and apologize for my actions. I still struggle sometimes to apologize to my wife, but God's example of grace through repenting helps me to focus on His faith instead of my failure.

Check out this promise about repenting and forgiveness.

> If we confess our sins, he is faithful and just and will
> forgive us our sins and purify us from all
> unrighteousness.
> 1 John 1:9

You see, this is the difference between Adam and us. When he sinned there had never been sin, so there was no atonement for it. There was and is nothing he or we can do to "earn" our way back into a no-sin state. This is where Jesus comes in to save the day for us. He is the atonement for our sins. It's why He had to die as a sacrifice for our redemption. So when we do sin, and confess it and repent, then only because of Christ Jesus we are placed back into a posture of good standing.

Man of Action Item 2:

The next action associated with being a Godly man is humility. It takes an incredible man to be a humble man. I thought I'd throw that one out there to make sure you were still plugged in. But in reality, if we think back to the most amazing people we knew or knew of, the one quality they all shared was humility. I'm not talking about a fake head nod and blush when you'd rather pound on your chest after making a great play or business deal.

Being humble is a spiritual gift for some, while it takes getting the snot beat out of life to humble others. Either way, men cannot come into a Christlike posture without a very healthy dose of being humble. I know in this Bro-eat-Bro world, it's hard to imagine getting yours without grabbing the spotlight and denying theirs, but take heed of another simple but timeless truth:

> Let someone else praise you, and not your own mouth;
>> an outsider, and not your own lips.
> Proverbs 27:2

I spent the first twenty-one years of my law enforcement career at a large, nationally accredited sheriff's office. Have you ever seen a bushel of live crabs? Every one of them is grabbing and clawing at the others to stop them from making it to the top, and possibly even escaping over the edge of the basket. Now, place several hundred alphas in an environment where testosterone pumps at full pressure, and watch them rip each other to shreds over a promotion, new vehicle assignment or pay raise.

There were many times I was tempted to shine a little light on myself just to get ahead of the pack, but instead, I invested my time encouraging, promoting and mentoring others. Guess what? I spent over twenty-three out of almost twenty-six years in a command capacity before becoming chief of police. Was I confident in my abilities? Sure was, but that was made possible because I understood what it meant to be humble among others.

Jesus had every right to expect praise for His miracles. The people wanted to crown Him king, but instead of allowing Himself to become the focus, He turned the focus on His Father. Yes, Jesus is as much God as is the Father, but He wasn't there for Himself. He was there so that you and me might come to know God the Father. Jesus came as a humble servant, and as an example of what a Godly man looks like.

Man of Action Item 3:

Servanthood is the third quality in learning to mirror God's image in ourselves. Jesus was the ultimate example of an incredibly powerful person who came to serve and not be served. Would you bow before others to wash their feet? I can't honestly say that I would, but that's why His example is so important for us to have as a model of true godliness.

Let's take a look at another verse that cuts to the core of what we should aspire to be:

> For even the Son of Man did not come to be served, but
>   to serve, and to give his life as a ransom for many.
> Mark 10:45

I know so many guys who say they'd give their life for their kids, and that's admirable. But would you give your life for someone you didn't know, or how about someone you didn't like? Here's a serious question, would you give your life for yourself? Why do I ask that? Because most of us have lived without taking ourselves into consideration. We can't serve others unless we first take care of ourselves.

Being a servant is having a willing heart to do for others above yourself. Don't worry if this doesn't come natural to you. As you pursue Christ and really make an effort to connect with Him, the Holy Spirit enters into the picture as Jesus' helper to develop your spirit-man over the worldly habits of your natural-man.

This in no way makes you any less of a man. Living a Godly life sometimes gets a bad rap from movies and media that love to portray a praying men as weak and unwilling to stand strong against adversity or the enemy. Do you recall God's charge for men in 1 Corinthians 16:13-14? And how about Jesus laying the law down when He busted up the corrupt dealers in the temple? There was no turning the other cheek when it came time to clean house in the righteous anger of condemnation.

Jesus entered the temple courts and drove out all who
were buying and selling there. He overturned the
tables of the money changers and the benches of
those selling doves. "It is written," he said to
them, "'My house will be called a house of prayer,' but
you are making it 'a den of robbers.'"
Matthew 21:12-13

I bet they didn't see that coming!!!

Man of Action Item 4:

This is a topic most want nothing to do with, but it's so vital to our Christian walk and the reality of the many consequences that result from a failure to practice sexual purity. If you're married, then go for it with your wife because God created sex as the covenant seal of marriage. It's designed to be fun and exciting.

I'm not sure who started that rumor about the missionary position being for believers, but while it's a good move, there are no restrictions on the expression of love between husband and wife. While there are boundaries, they are meant as guidelines to protect what is valuable in your marriage and sexual relationship:

- Sex is only between you and your wife. No other people, porn or mental fantasies of others.
- Is it mutually pleasurable for the both of you?
- Anything goes as long as both of you consent to it.

Now, if you're not married, I know it's a tough decision to remain sexually pure. I've been straight with you throughout, so you know that when I became sexually active at age twelve, it led to chaos, destruction and more harm than I may ever realize. It was a drug just like any other substance used to dull pain or hopelessly fill a void.

Sexual sin can lead to unwanted pregnancies, unaffordable child support, divorce, abortion, disease, death, poverty, addiction and so many other life-altering circumstances that remain beyond our control, for the sake of what? Think about your best sexual activity ever. Now compare that to a lifetime of paying for a child out of marriage, or medications for an incurable STD. Is it really worth those fleeting moments of physical stimulation?

I had no idea what I was doing to my mind, body and spirit. I was like so many other men and thought having consensual, noncommitted sex was just what guys did. When we look at what the apostle Paul said about sexual immorality, it highlights the severity of playing the field. He doesn't say walk, flirt or think about it. He says to flee!!

> Flee from sexual immorality. All other sins a person
> commits are outside the body, but whoever sins
> sexually, sins against their own body.
> 1 Corinthians 6:18

I cover sexual temptation and breaking the chains of addiction in other books I've authored, so if this is something that hits home, you might want to check that out next.

Let me leave you with this word from God, and again, this has taken me years to understand and a focused effort to overcome. I pray that your journey to freedom from sexual sin is much quicker than mine. Sexual purity may not be popular locker room talk, but it is your direct path to freedom and God's great blessings.

> Therefore, I urge you, brothers and sisters, in view of
> God's mercy, to offer your bodies as a living
> sacrifice, holy and pleasing to God—this is your true
> and proper worship. Do not conform to the pattern
> of this world, but be transformed by the renewing of
> your mind. Then you will be able to test and approve
> what God's will is—his good, pleasing and perfect
> will.
> Romans 12:1-2

Man of Action Item 5:

A man of action is also a leader by example. In my years of law enforcement, I worked within a rigidly structured chain of command. I can tell you there were many sergeants, lieutenants, captains, majors and such that might've worn insignia on their collar, but they failed to bear the weight of leadership. I always understood that if you have to tell people you're in charge, then you really aren't in charge.

Being a Godly man is the same way. It's the light of Christ that shines from within your soul that attracts people to you. Of course, when that same light is diminished by sin, people are also repelled by what they see in the way you live. You become transparent to others when you say one thing but do the other. It's called being a living sacrifice and witness for Christ. Be a positive example to others by leading in your words and actions.

> Don't let anyone look down on you because you are
> young, but set an example for the believers in speech,
> in conduct, in love, in faith and in purity.
> 1 Timothy 4:12

Man of Action Item 6:

This last action item is a quick catchall, but it captures the heart of what each of the above items share, and extends beyond what life lived in the valley of darkness can bring. There is light in life with Christ. God is calling, pleading, almost begging for men to rise up to be His ambassadors. He wants to bless you, but He must first know that you can be trusted with the blessing.

Being a Godly man is being a man of action. Pursuing, pressing and patiently praying for all things in His time and opportunity is what actual action is about. Pursue a relationship with the Holy Spirit. Too often we don't understand the nature of the Spirit, so we overlook the connection. God is what is called Triune. It means He is one God in three equal parts, but each of the three always equals one: the Father, the Son and the Holy Spirit.

There is no boss over the others, although there is submission to one another. God the Father promised us Jesus the Son to share the good news of the gospel of salvation. Jesus came to us as a man to share His new testament of grace and mercy as opposed to the restrictive Mosaic laws. In His coming, Jesus also submitted to die as an atonement for our sins.

In His crucifixion, Jesus sent us the Holy Spirit to be our guide and helper until the time that Christ returns. The Holy Spirit is God and is what lives inside of us when we open our heart to Christ. Ever get that warm fuzzy feeling, or the cool chill when sin is at hand, and also when you get quiet and still? How about when you stand in the shower as tears flood your face? Maybe the times when you feel overwhelming emotion when there's no reason to feel anything? Or when you find yourself all alone, yet you feel completely at peace in the silence?

Yep, that's the Holy Spirit. Get to know Him, Bro.

Since we live by the Spirit, let us keep in step with the
Spirit.
Galatians 5:25

Not Being Perfect

My Brother, a Godly man is not perfect, but we do celebrate our manhood and know that Christ sets the gold standard for how we will live. It's not like we can set the spiritual-man on autopilot and glide through Godly living. We'll work daily to model our actions after Jesus. Honestly, we'll struggle moment by moment just to get by or avoid a satanic-fueled temptation to throw us, but in that struggle we grow stronger. Confessing our sins, asking God to forgive us and renewing our commitment is a continual cycle that spins us closer to Christ.

No matter what we look like, how much money we do or don't make, married, divorced or single, whether we've got one friend or one million followers on social media, you can purposefully choose be a Godly man if you give your life over to God. Living a Godly life is being the ultimate alpha male just like God the Father. That life is waiting for you, if you'll just trust Him.

> So he answered and said, "'You shall love the Lord your
> God with all your heart, with all your soul, with all
> your strength, and with all your mind,' and 'your
> neighbor as yourself.'"
> Luke 10:27

Helping It Happen

My first title for this section was Making It Happen, but then I realized how selfish and contrary it was to what we're talking about. Making it happen implies we did it on our own, and of course, that leads to arrogance and pride. God makes it crystal clear how He feels about pride:

> To fear the Lord is to hate evil; I hate pride and
> arrogance, evil behavior and perverse speech.
> Proverbs 8:13

The Godly perspective is in understanding that while God loves to bless us, we are still expected to put in the work. Ever seen those guys in the gym who live with shredded abs yet never do a single sit-up? I know, I can't stand them either, but the truth is, they are blessed genetically. Does that mean they still don't have to put in the effort or at least watch what they eat? Sure they do, and if they did more than show up, who knows the physical potential they might tap into.

It's the same thing with this book and these man of action items. You can read over them and allow them to blow like a Gulf breeze through the Bahama blinds, or you can claim them as power over your life. They do have life-changing potential, and just like ab exercises in the gym, how ripped you want your spiritual life to become depends on how much work you're willing to put in. I'm serious when I tell you that these few simple action items will change your life.

5

WHAT'S TROUBLING US?

"War is hell," General William Tecumseh Sherman famously said about his Civil War experience. It was, is and always will be hell, and guess what? We men are at war with the world. Well, to be more specific, at war with liberal ideologies opposed to the nature of manhood.

The latest emotional demands require that we wave a white flag of surrender and dilute the testosterone that makes us different into a dangerous solution of sameness. Men and women are absolutely equal, but we are definitely not the same.

Toxic masculinity is their battle cry!

My first, and natural-man response was once, "Bring it on." But as I understood God's mercy and grace as it had saved my life, I started to see that being an alpha male isn't toxic in and of itself. Where the toxicity comes from is in the pain we carry because of being hurt by other people, and yes, mostly other men. Toxicity is continually pressed upon us through cycles of domination, abuse, addiction, abandonment, and all around acting like a prick on occasion.

How'd we find ourselves the target of social outrage? After all, it's been us who built, bought and conquered to create the world everyone gets to enjoy while they criticize us for what we've sacrificed for them. Unfortunately, we've also fought, raped and pillaged our way across history in search of the power to build, buy and conquer the world. But that history, just like your past, doesn't have to define us now or going forward.

Battle On

Let's take the gloves off and get right down to smacking slabs of hung rib meat like Stallone did in *Rocky 6* or *7* or *21* or...

I want to jump into what's hanging over our heads. While I don't think the truth is going to devastate you, I do think the purposeful effort against us men might surprise you. We've given up lots of ground over the last few decades. Not that we were engaged in a land battle of the sexes, but to be honest, while we were being neutered by secular, anti-men policies, we might've found ourselves beneath a high heel across our masculine necks.

Also during this time, an entirely new crop of options have emerged under the guise of shifting identification for gender based on that morning's mood. This may be a bailout for you, but there are the same two genders today that were first created in the garden: male and female.

And while you may be a "live and let live" kinda guy, you might want to know that the only ones not being allowed to let live are us. Equality is the goal, but in the war on masculinity, there is no living in harmony with the enemy, otherwise known as the alpha male.

Yeah, I feel like Encino Man. How about you?

So, how did the neutering happen? I mean wouldn't you think we'd have at least gotten an email, or raised an objection? It started before we were born, so don't beat yourself up for failing to be battle ready. It's been steady and stealthy for decades up until recently when the mainstream media decided it was time to openly declare war.

Mix and Match

Maybe it's just me, but moving a step back and taking an honest inventory of what is going on around us can be a bit overwhelming. Nowadays, right is wrong and wrong is a ticket to riches.

Protectors are evil because they pursue the wolves, but the wolves are the ones society shows support to if they are captured or injured while ravaging their prey. Work is bad because entitlement is good. Honesty is no longer the best policy because political correctness and anti-accountability is preferred.

We could go on and on, but why waste the beats of our heart recounting what we can log onto social media to see for ourselves. No matter how much society tries to force change, living on its shifting ideological sand is never a good idea.

Trying to go alone in these tumultuous times is unwise. We've got God as our general to not only guide us through but to actually go ahead of us to fight our battles. But we've still got to up our alpha game.

But why, you may still ask. I asked the same question many times through the years. I was content with who I was and the life I was living. Like I said before, I was well accomplished in my career, had earned the highest academic status awarded and proven myself a formidable sportsman.

What was missing?

Relationship is what was missing. Although I had no idea, the truth was I was missing the most important relationship in life—the relationship with God. Sure, I'd usually remember to give Him a shout-out before meals or when things in life got really rocky.

But I was living life for no one but me. After I did it, only then did I expect God to be okay with it. And since I was unaware or unwilling to admit that I needed that close spiritual relationship, I struggled in the tough times when instead I should've been able to Man Up.

Let's dig deeper.

6

THE ADAM LIFE

Living the Adam life?

I remember back in school after coming off of our first loss in the basketball season, our coach huddled us at center court. We were sad over that loss, but we were also afraid of what would come out of his mouth. We'd disappointed our beloved mentor. He looked like an ancient oak, and when he spoke, his thunderous words cracked like lightning tipped with wisdom.

He said, "Boys, we're going back to the basics."

That was it. I wasn't even sure what the basics were, but I understood we'd failed to execute them during that game. I also understood they were going to be the most important thing to us because it was important to our coach. It also happened to be the last game we'd lose that year, or the next.

What we need to look at is going back to the basics. And by the basics, I mean the beginning—the very beginning. Whether you know it, we've not moved the needle very far from Adam. Yep, that Adam. The very first man—the alpha male. Think I'm nuts? Let's take a look.

The Adam Life

I was living the Adam life. I believed in God, and spent time in prayer while enjoying a relationship with Him. I even sensed God's presence as He walked me through good times and bad. But when the chips were on the table and I had an opportunity to show my love for Him, I bit the apple. I bit it a lot. And often.

How many of us live that same Adam life every day? We want to do good, and we promise that we will be good, but too often we drop the ball. I'm not making an excuse for you or me, but the reality is, it's in our DNA.

Don't sell yourself short by using the H-card. You know the one we pull out whenever we could have and should have done the right thing, but for about a million reasons, we didn't. Yes, the tired old, "I'm only human," alibi is yesterday's news. It doesn't sell today, so trash it.

We are indeed human, but in that humanity we were created in the image of perfection. God said it Himself. We covered it before, but if you need a quick refresher on how awesome you were created to be, look at Genesis 1:26.

God said, "Let us make mankind in our image, in our likeness, so that they may rule over the fish in the sea and the birds in the sky, over the livestock and all the wild animals, and over all the creatures that move along the ground."

For now, though, let's focus on what went down between the garden and today. There's a lot of history we could sift through to come up with endless explanations, but how about we cut to the heart of it?

Sin

The one consistency throughout history is man's sin behavior. Sin separated Adam from God. Sin kept His chosen people out of the Promised Land. With the exception of Noah's family, sin condemned the entire human population to death. Sin caused entire cities like Sodom and Gomorrah to perish. Sin caused educated and religious leaders to refute and crucify the promised Messiah. And, sin has caused you and me misery and pain throughout our lives.

This is what has happened to man: sin. God truly wants to bless us with more than our natural minds can imagine. Yet we're so afraid. Yes, I said the "A" word. We'd rather skid through the muck of what life allows than grab the glory that the King is bursting to bestow upon us.

Although we were meant for blessings, as a whole, we've done a crummy job living the life God once and still desires for each of us. Our lineage from Adam is littered with us taking the moral, ethical and spiritual plunge.

Yeah, but what about…

We'll look at biblical heroes and the negative effects of their sin nature. We're also going to look at the redemptive value of forgiveness and renewal despite the fact that these men were only human.

I'm not going to blast these guys, but it's important for you to see that those who stood tallest had to first be picked up off their behinds. God didn't stick with them because of their misdeeds, but because He knew the desires of their hearts. And yes, they wanted to do good, but like most of us, they didn't know how.

Did Adam Doom Us?

That's a fair question, and if you choose to live under the action of the first Adam, then yes, you're pretty much a sunk duck. Why? Because nothing you can do, no amount of money you can pay or weight you can overhead press is ever going to be good enough to earn your way back into God's good standing. Why? Because God gave you the way back—Jesus.

It's like me giving you free tickets to the Super Bowl. All you have to do is accept the fifty-yard-line seats, and I'll take care of the rest. Instead, you reject them and decide you'll get into the game another way. Can you imagine trying to sneak past Super Bowl security? There's no such thing. You'll spend the game in jail or just out in the cold. Same thing with rejecting God's free gift to the biggest, best event in history.

You're not doomed. Even if your life up to this very moment has been junk, it doesn't have to continue to be so. I lived with so much misery that for years I kept a loaded .357 by the nightstand just in case I woke up and couldn't think of one good reason to go on. You know what? God fed me reason after reason each and every day until I finally realized that I could stop nibbling on excuses, and instead feast on a banquet of His blessings.

But you have a choice to make. Do you accept the free gift of grace, or do you continue crawling through the pain, disappointment and darkness from one decent emotion to the next?

Maybe it's a good time to offer another "bailout." There are folks who refuse to believe they sin, or think that the good work they do will save them a spot in the heavenly above. There was only one perfect person, and we crucified Him.

I'll hate to see you stop here, but if there is the deceptive seed of placing yourself equal to or above God the creator, then this might be the perfect place to say, "See you later."

> For by grace you have been saved through faith, and that
> not of yourselves; it is the gift of God, not of works,
> lest anyone should boast
> Ephesians 2:8-9

Still with me? Great decision, my Brother.

We're all sinners and as you know, the wages of sin is death, but by simply believing in Christ, we are saved. You don't gain and lose salvation like a hot streak at the roulette table. But in case you're firing up a big old mess of sin, God commands us to sin no more.

My sheep hear My voice, and I know them and they
follow Me. And I give them eternal life, and they shall
never perish; neither shall anyone snatch them out of
My hand.
John 10:27-28

Bigger Better Deal

We've been picking on Adam harder than a freshman at a frat rush party. He was *el numero uno*. He had no student loans, no baby mommas, no slow Wi-Fi or worries about next year's fantasy football picks. This guy was God's +1, and he was the very first global CEO. Seriously, the guy had it all.

But, just like us, he wanted more. Adam wanted the bigger, better deal. Whether it's making a quarter more an hour at the new job, the hotter girlfriend or the first-six-months-free cable packages, we want more. So did Adam, and we're still paying for his selfish power grab.

Adam spoke directly with God, and yet he still stumbled. We also have direct access to God, but we also find ways to stumble as well. Brother, don't buy into the religious hype that only professional priests or pastors can talk to God. The pope is no more able to talk to God than you or me. The depth and sincerity of the communications depends on our heart for God.

If we're willing to listen, we will hear God speak as clearly to us as He did with Adam. When the word gets fuzzy is because we started adding filters to the listening process. God told His #1 boy to enjoy everything in paradise. So God put Adam in the garden to work it, and to keep it up so that he could enjoy the fruits of his labor.

Then He very clearly told Adam that it was okay to eat from any tree in the garden except for one very specific tree. As much as God loved Adam, He made no bones about it, and if His main man ate from that one tree, then he'd die.

> The Lord God took the man and put him in the garden
> of Eden to work it and keep it. And the Lord God
> commanded the man, saying, "You may surely eat of
> every tree of the garden, but of the tree of the
> knowledge of good and evil you shall not eat, for in
> the day that you eat of it you shall surely die."
> Genesis 2:15-17

Did you know that in the very beginning, man wasn't designed to die? We weren't created to be sick or depressed, or addicted or divorced or any of the things we suffer today. It was sin that gave us what we get today. When God tells Adam that he will die, He meant it in a physical death, and in a spiritual death through separation from Him. What happens if you cut a branch off of a tree, or a finger off of your hand? Yep, apart from the body, it will die.

As you know, Adam bit from that fruit. Now, before we start dropping criticism bombs about how could he have screwed up so bad since he was so close to God, guess what? Adam was no more or less loved by God than God loves you and me. Adam walked with Him, and so do you and I. There is no difference between the garden of Eden that Adam walked in and ours.

Let me explain. Eden can become a complicated concept. Historians have searched for the physical garden, which was an actual spot on earth. More importantly the word Eden equals presence, as in God's presence. So when Adam walked in the garden of Eden, he was walking on earth, with and within God's presence. Let me take another swing at the piñata.

God is omniscient, omnipotent and omnipresent, which means He's twenty-four/seven everywhere, every time. No matter what you do, where you go or what's in your heart, God is there with you— Eden. But because our original big brother bit that fruit, we all lost direct access to God's presence, but not access to God.

Instead of throwing stones at our very first alpha dog, how about instead we accept that we've not progressed far from where Adam was in the days of Eden. Look, sin is sin, Bro. Adam bit a piece of fruit, and his son Cain murdered his brother, Abel. Both sins resulted in exile and separation from God (spiritual death).

So how about us, men? What's your sin? Adultery, porn, alcohol, drugs, violence, greed, lust, pride, theft, covetousness, refusing to forgive others, your dad or yourself? You see, we do walk with God, we have gotten His word of instruction, and yes still, we bite what is forbidden.

Do you see the pattern? It stretches from the very first man up to possibly you, and definitely me. I guess it'd be easy to say God messed up on the entire batch of what He called man. But you know better than that, because we are restored through faith as His perfect creation.

So now you ask, "If God loves us, why did He let Adam sin?"

Great question. God loves us so much that instead of condemning us to walking about the earth chewing cud like His other creations, He gave man free will and an ability to think and reason. Unfortunately, it was this free will that also set our path down the road of generational failure.

I'll give it to you from another angle. If you were in a relationship but forced to stay with her because of threats or blackmail, how deep would your love run? Instead, if you were encouraged to stay only if you wanted to, but were also free to leave if it made you happier, then how would it make you feel? Free will isn't a license to run wild, it's a loving permission to freely choose.

It's only when our will is in alignment with God that we rise above subjecting ourselves to instantaneous personal whims and temporary physical desires. I'm sure I don't have to connect these dots to what we call sin. Anything outside of what God intimately desires for us leads to sin. It's not a control power trip, but it is that all He wants is what is good and best for us.

Don't let that throw you. You're not supposed to live your life inside a repressed box of rules and regulations. God wants a full and plentiful existence for you—a blessed life. Most of the rules that push you away from God are not of God. They are man-made rituals created to place God into a nice little box where we can visit Him on Sundays when we're on our best behavior. That is not God.

The Judean prophet Jeremiah assured us of this even during one of the more difficult times in Jerusalem's history.

> "For I know the plans I have for you," declares the Lord,
> "plans to prosper you and not to harm you, plans to
> give you hope and a future."
> Jeremiah 29:11

Take a second and go back to read that. I'm sometimes guilty of halfway skimming over Bible verses in text, but I'm asking for a second look because there's a blessing for you within God's simple promise. If you think it's too late, or you've messed up too bad or that God can't use you, you're flat mistaken. God says He has plans for you. Plans to prosper you. Not to harm you. Plans for hope. Plans for a future. How clear is that?

These are the words I want you to think about. You have the authority to do one of two things with words like these; you can reject them and they'll die on the vine; or you can accept them and allow them to speak prophetic words of power over your life. Which do you choose?

My Brother, it doesn't matter what your life looks like right now. If it's a mess, God will use it as a message. God loves you, and whatever it is that you're going through right now is not His punishment. Your circumstances are His platform, and if you allow Him to do His work in and through you, then each and every word of Jeremiah 29:11 will live out in you through His promise to you.

So, I'll ask you again, "Which do you choose?"

The Second Adam?

I've mentioned terms like natural-man and spiritual-man so far, but other than assuming we're on the same page, I haven't clarified either. We have two natures. The one we're most in tune with is our natural being. It would be hard not to be, right? We wake up with him, shower, shave and feed him all day, every day.

It's our natural-man that usually guides us through life, and yep, often into trouble because our natural man is focused on getting through the grind of daily life while serving himself as often as possible, i.e....biting the apple.

Our other nature is our spirit-man. He's the gift of life from God. The spirit-man is right there with you, except he's not like your natural man who makes demands for food, fun and fiestas. Your spirit man is cool, and knows best, but he's not going to force you to do anything no matter how good it is for you.

I guess your spirit-man is kinda like a grandmother when it comes to eating your veggies. She'll make 'em, but she won't make you sit there until you eat them like Mom or Dad will.

So what's the point? It goes back to free will. God loves you and just like Adam, He gives clear instruction so that you may enjoy Eden in all of its pleasure. But He won't force you to avoid the tree, or the strip club, or the alcohol and drugs or the sex and porn.

You ask again, what's the point? Well, it's your choice whether to serve the natural-man's desires of this world, or to pursue the spirit-man's heart for things above. If your life is in chaos, and it's time to get your act together, then consider the difference between following the same serpent that led Adam astray, or the Jesus who only wants what's best in your life.

So if things aren't as you might want them to be, then don't sweat it because there's a pattern of the spirit-man following the natural-man for the sake of making things right. Adam, who was the natural-man just like us, came first, but as we've discussed, kinda messed up.

Jesus, on the other hand, also came as a man, but was in the spirit realm. As a result, He didn't fall for the same evil temptations as the natural-man once did. That didn't mean He came to gloat, but to redeem the natural-man by making the ultimate sacrifice for all of the sins of the world since our prototype big brother, Adam.

So to clear up the logic of natural versus spiritual, I'll refer to 1 Corinthians 15:45-48 because it shares exactly the story of how the first Adam came from the earth (natural) without sin, but fell to temptation, and that Jesus, the second Adam, came of the spirit, remained without blemish as an atonement for the sins of the world.

> So it is written: "The first man Adam became a living being" the last Adam, a life-giving spirit. The spiritual did not come first, but the natural, and after that the spiritual. The first man was of the dust of the earth, the second man from heaven. As was the earthly man, so are those who are of the earth; and as is the man from heaven, so also are those who are of heaven.
> 1 Corinthians 15:45-48

In other words, God's got our back!

7

FIVE PILLARS OF A GODLY MAN

Because we're men, it's not like us to pad around in small circles with both hands shoved in our pockets. It's time to move forward and get things done. So now that we've taken an honest look at where we've been, let's avoid repeating history, and gain some positive ground.

We've talked about alpha males in terms such as natural-man and the spirit-man, and this is an important distinction in the journey. I'm going to go over five pillars for the spirit-man that are vital to the foundation of building that better man. If we focus on what God has for our lives through changes on the inside, then His light will naturally shine through us toward the outside.

I've prayed over each of these building blocks in your plan to crafting the better man. Each one is meaningful as a mentoring guide for your path.

All are scripture based and just like a prophetic word spoken over your life, you have the authority to claim it and proclaim its power over your future, or you may allow it to flutter overhead like a missed end zone pass. The authority is yours.

Spirit-Man

The spirit-man is the reflection of God's light shining through us. We all have a natural-man, or our body. That's what walks around all day, hangs out with friends, goes for his best bench press max on Monday evening, and chooses to serve God and others, or not.

We also all have a soul, which is what God breathed into Adam's nostrils to bring the physical frame to life. Your soul is your thoughts, feelings, free will, emotions, memories and all of the things that make us different from some droid on an assembly line.

Thirdly, we have a spirit-man inside of us. Now, this is where reality gets raw, and maybe a good time for a bailout. If you don't believe that satan is real, then this next part is going to rub you very much in the wrong way.

I'd hate to see you ring that bell, but there is no neutral ground in this supernatural realm. God makes no bones about satan, and he is not some silly cartoon with horns and a tail. Actually, satan will come to you as the thing you think you need most at your most needy time. He can be alcohol, porn, drugs, sex or suicide, but one thing he cannot be is anything beyond his sin nature.

> So the great dragon was cast out, that serpent of old,
>   called the Devil and Satan, who deceives the whole
>   world; he was cast to the earth, and his angels were
>   cast out with him.
> Revelation 12:9

So back to our spirit-man; we all have one, but which team your spirit is on depends on whether you've given your life to God or not. If Jesus is not lord over your life, then by default, the devil is. You can't straddle this fence.

Some men think they can reserve an empty booth in the back of the Christian Café and when they're tired of dancing with the devil, a seat will be open. If the devil took you to the ball, chances are you will be going home with him. Unless, of course, you make the commitment to Christ. This is why we'll focus on the spirit-man to share building blocks for the better man.

Pillar 1: PRAYER

> One day Jesus was praying in a certain place. When he
> finished, one of his disciples said to him, "Lord, teach
> us to pray, just as John taught his disciples."
> Luke 11:1

Have you ever been on a road trip with a friend and you never run out of stuff to talk about? It's the way God once hung out with Adam; it's the way He wants to hang out with us. Prayer is simply communicating with God. The Bible tells us to pray without ceasing, just like the way conversation flows with your best bud.

I know it sounds weird, but so did the idea of video phone calls long before FaceTime. Prayer makes the relationship real, and the first step in building the better man is getting in touch with the construction's supervisor.

Unfortunately, we aren't quick to hit our knees in prayer. I struggled with it for years, and even when I wanted to get closer, I felt like there was a brick wall between us. Of course, the issue wasn't because God didn't want to hang out, it was totally on my end. I came to understand a few hang-ups we have, and I want to cover them so you don't feel like you're all alone if praying doesn't come naturally.

1. I don't know how to pray or what to say.

Yep, this is a big one. Most men feel intimidated at the idea of even saying grace over a meal. Forget the rituals and recitals that some religions teach you or instruct you to count beads or repeat Hail Marys to get out of the confessional outhouse. That's not prayer.

God wants to hear your voice because what's in your heart is reflected through the power of your words. I tell men all of the time to just start talking, and the Holy Spirit will help you with the rest. This is also not the time to pull any punches with God. Remember, He knows you better than you know yourself. The idea behind chatting with Him is that you come to know Him as well as you better understanding yourself.

2. I don't know many or any Bible verses, and I might sound dumb?

I used to dread opening my mouth to pray. So much so, that it caused serious issues in my marriage. I didn't sound like Billy Graham, and I was worried what God would think of me for not speaking religious and eloquent. You guessed it. I'm a basic blue-collar guy, so if I began with flowery speeches about bountiful blessings, God would've tuned out because that wasn't the condition of my heart.

Also, don't sweat reciting Bible verses. He already knows them because they are His words. It would be like talking to your friend about a movie and being expected to only recite the show's script. God doesn't want a repeat, He wants a relationship. That takes honest, open conversation, not Bible verse regurgitation.

3. I'm afraid I might say something wrong.

God says that there is only one unforgivable sin, and that is blaspheming the Holy Spirit. Don't go there and be sure that there is nothing you can say that God considers wrong. If this is the case, then I'd guess you, just like I did, still have unconfessed sin.

One of the main reasons I avoided praying with my wife was because I still kept secrets from her. I was afraid something would slip out while I was being a holy man—a fake holy man. If you're not willing to open yourself up to the very one who created you and died for you, then there may be something you really do need to talk to God about—unconfessed sin.

4. I don't have time.

Seriously? This is the response I try not to give when guys tell me they don't have time to pray. We want eternal life, yet we can't spare a minute or two? Read this aloud:

"God, I need you."

No, really, read that aloud. You don't have to scream it, but you do at least have to allow it to roll off your tongue. Okay, that is what we call a prayer. Albeit a short one, but still a prayer. Unbelievers have been saved into glory just seconds before their own death with "God, save me," or something similar. It's not the word count, but the words that count. Talk from your heart and allow yourself to see you in a brand-new light.

5. I'm afraid of what might happen if I do pray.

I completely understand. It's intimidating to know that one simple act can have a life-changing effect. If you're struggling with an addiction, then you know that reality of how that first drink, hit or web click changed your life. This change is a good change. Actually, it's great!

Prayer comes with God's blessings, but also requires spiritual responsibility. It's like the old expression, "You kiss your mother with that mouth?" God isn't a magic lamp we rub when we're in a fix. Prayer is a process, and a lifestyle, and it's definitely not something to be afraid of.

6. I've tried to pray but God isn't listening.

Have you ever prayed, but felt like your words didn't get past the ceiling? And no, the answer is not to go outside to pray, it's to search your soul for unrepentant sin. Sin separates us from God, just like we've covered earlier in Romans 6:23—*"For the wages of sin is death."*

Our words bouncing back from the ceiling isn't because God is mad at us, it's because He cannot look at us if we're stained by unconfessed sin. When Jesus called out from the cross, *"My God, my God, why have you forsaken me?"* (Mark 15:34), God had not forsaken His beloved Son, but at that moment, Jesus had taken on every sin of the world for our atonement. God loved Him as He loves you, but His nature doesn't allow sin to enter the relationship.

I'll wrap up this part about prayer with a word about making it a part of your daily life. If you sincerely want to make an awesome, blessed life for yourself, and build that better man, then make the time to pray every day.

There are no corners to cut—get to know God and He will show you the you that you could've never imagined. I know that was using the word *you* probably way too often, but who cares!!! This is you we're talking about, and you're freaking awesome.

Pillar 2: COMMITMENT

I have fought the good fight, I have finished the race, I have kept the faith.
2 Timothy 4:7

While I've been told I should be committed, this isn't the type of committed we're talking about. Oh, and those that say it, are among friends who are only joking. I hope. But seriously, commitment is so critical in the process of building the better man. The mere act of committing to complete this book shows you where you are in the process of sticking to something. Focus is a big part of commitment, and wow, have we become conditioned to fall short on focus.

When I think how differently this section would've been written less than a decade ago before the social media explosion, it blows my mind. I'd have never imagined while mentoring men, I'd have to ask them to put down their cell phones and commit to simply paying attention. That is, unless you're reading this on your cell phone.

The simplest commitment we can make is to get our heads out of social media and invest in the actual world around us. I've had to stop briefings for dangerous police missions because officers were preoccupied with social media. No one is immune, nor does it discriminate based on socioeconomic demographics.

Did you know that in 70 percent of divorce pleadings nationwide, Facebook is mentioned as one of the grievances? Can you imagine a voluntary-participation, virtual social application causing so much real-life misery? Why: because we are unable to commit. Whether it's a marriage, parenting responsibility, friendship, work, hobby, health or faith, we're losing the ability to stick to it.

We have historically lived a what's-up-next type of life. Easily distracted, quickly deterred and suddenly disinterested, we allow these impediments to cover every aspect of our life. Often to our own misfortune. Whether it's worship, wife or work, we're off to the next big thing without a thought of the commitment we'd made to the prior.

Let us not lose heart in doing good, for in due time we
will reap if we do not grow weary.
Galatians 6:9

It's so important to be a man of our word. Even if it causes us to take a loss of time or money. If we agreed to something, we've got to stick to our guns. Commitment is a sign of character, and more importantly, it reflects the nature of God from us onto others.

God Made Man encourages you to commit to reading each section and giving it the time to meditate over the words that pierce your spirit. It's not because my writing is stellar, but because I commit to write only what God puts on my heart. I've made a spiritual commitment to you, and as an alpha male, I'd appreciate you making the same level of commitment to building the better man.

It usually takes three weeks to develop a habit, so commit to praying every day, or reading your bible, or watching your favorite pastor's video series. Just start by making a commitment to something.

If you commit daily by making the time to focus on prayer, reading or learning God's Word, you will experience a gradual but dynamic change in your life. What that change looks like depends on what it is that you are dealing with in life.

Often, we fail to follow through, even if it means busting through whatever it is that has burdened you. We change focus for the sake of shifting lanes to avoid the hassle. That doesn't get us to our destination; it only sends us out of our path to destiny. Did you realize that your blessing is right on the other side of your burden? God places your blessing into your future so that once you progress past where you are now, there is something special waiting just down the tracks.

For I know the plans I have for you, declares the Lord,
plans for welfare and not for evil, to give you a future
and a hope.
Jeremiah 29:11

Let's consider the example of committing set by Jesus. He came with a laser-vision focus on delivering the good news of the gospel. There were so many opportunities for Him to have said, "Enough," and ascended back to paradise. But, although He knew the violent ending to His ministry of salvation, He remained committed to the mission.

I've skipped leg workouts at the gym because I knew how much squats were going to hurt! Does that mean I'll never be Christlike? No, it means I still have room to grow in the commitment department, and in the gym!

God's commitments throughout the Old Testament span over generations, and across the globe. His word was given to a single person, and held the power of affecting millions of lives, or just one.

God is good, and good for His word. Imagine committing to the birth of a child to a ninety-year-old woman? Even Sarah had to laugh at that one, but just as God committed that she'd give birth, there came baby Isaac.

God's commitments to us have been the foundation for the rise of nations, and the lineage from His promise to Abraham, all the way to the royal bloodline of Jesus. Has God reconsidered His commitment to us? Sure, He's grown disappointed in our wickedness, and wanted to wipe out the whole thing. But He's good to His word, and yet here we are. Thankfully.

> "Let Me alone, that I may destroy them and blot out
>   their name from under heaven."
> Deuteronomy 9:14

That's pretty serious stuff right there. But what happens is that Moses, who loved and pursued the heart of God, reminded Him of His commitment. Even in God's righteous anger, He defaulted to keeping His word, and His very commitment.

"Turn from your fierce anger; relent and do not bring
disaster on your people. Remember your servants
Abraham, Isaac and Israel, to whom you swore by
your own self: 'I will make your descendants as
numerous as the stars in the sky and I will give your
descendants all this land I promised them, and it will
be their inheritance forever.'" Then
the Lord relented and did not bring on his people the
disaster he had threatened.
Exodus 32:12-14

It's normal that we get tired, irritated or uninterested in following through on a commitment. Maybe we don't feel like meeting our workout partner at the CrossFit box, or go to that dinner party we promised our wife, but being a Godly man means keeping our word and commitment. When we fail to commit, it not only diminishes our Christ-nature for reliability, but it negatively affects those we committed to.

Commit to keeping your word.

Pillar 3: FORGIVING

Be kind to one another, tenderhearted, forgiving one another,
as God in Christ forgave you.
Ephesians 4:32

There are so many terms that reflect the character of Christ, and forgiving easily found itself in our five pillars for better man building. I know from the men I've talked to in preparing to write this book that their and maybe your, first reaction was "Huh?"

Not that you don't know what forgiving means, but it's so often misunderstood why not refresh. We, men, aren't good at forgiving from the biblical standard. Sure, we'll tell our wife, or a friend who has offended us, that, "Yeah, we're cool. No big deal," but it is a big deal, and brushing them off isn't the same thing as forgiving them.

God is pretty clear that forgiving others is a huge deal. He also doesn't pull punches with the caveat that if you do not forgive others, He will not forgive you. This is the exact same place Adam found himself when banished from God's presence.

> But if you do not forgive others their sins, your Father
>   will not forgive your sins.
> Matthew 6:15

A Godly man forgives. And when he's offended again, he forgives again. Now, I know you might think that makes us look weak, but it's only weak without an understanding of what forgiving really is. Forgiveness doesn't mean we approve of what wrong someone has done to us. It means we have the authority to release ourselves from that person and their harmful act.

Refusing to forgive is like allowing someone to hold a leash while you bark and run around the yard in circles, yanking against the chain. They have hold and control of you, but forgiving them is you taking their tether off of your neck, laying it on the ground and walking away, free.

Even Jesus' main man Peter had an issue with the idea of unlimited and unconditional forgiveness. He tried to pull a fast one with what he thought was a trick question. In their time, forgiving someone three times was considered excellent.

Peter used the three times, and as an extra measure of being a righteous dude, he doubled it and added one. Jesus wasn't buying it. He corrected His friend and assured him that we are to forgive not seven times, but seventy times seven. That doesn't mean we forgive them 490 times and then they're condemned.

That number meant we are to forgive an unlimited amount of times. Just think if we were limited to only 490 forgivings through our life?

Tough to Forgive

Let's talk about tough. Jesus was nailed to a cross after having been whipped, beaten and marched to His place of crucifixion. As He hung on that wooden cross, legions of angels were available at His command to swoop in and destroy everyone who opposed Him. But what did this ultimate tough guy do?

He looked at those who delighted in His torture, those who mocked His pain and those who swore loyalty but denied Him otherwise. He had the power to take revenge on all of them. Instead, Jesus asked His Father to forgive them because they didn't have a clue what they were doing. He did what we must do, and forgave them.

> Jesus said, "Father, forgive them, for they do not know
> what they are doing..."
> Luke 23:34

I'll admit one of my strongholds was that I would not forgive. I used to say that I couldn't do it, but that was my selfish attitude of judgment against others, and myself. Sure I could. I just chose not to, and it ate at me every day.

God smacked me with an undeniable message that it was way past time to heal. I realized that I was in so much pain, and like scraping a burn scab off, I just continued to open and reinjure myself.

But as tough as I thought it was, I began to pray out loud the names of the people who hurt me. In private, I began to speak out loud that I forgave them by name. We don't even have to say it to the person, or if they've already passed away, we just need to speak the words because God wants to hear our voice as He already knows our heart.

I kept doing this in the privacy of my home, and as each day passed, I began to rage less and less about what they'd done to hurt me. I eventually realized that I wasn't angry, I wasn't thinking about them all day, and I definitely wasn't in pain over the past.

Soon, God showed me what it was to be free. I was completely free for the first time in years. Then came the next step in building the better me. God not only calls us to forgive others, but to bless them. If we truly believe in Christ, how could we not ask God to bless them with His merciful act of salvation? Yes, even those who have hurt us.

Manning Up isn't about lying down. It's about having the courage, commitment and supernatural understanding to see that we aren't fighting against other people, but that our battles are on a higher plane. Forgiving and blessing our enemies makes us warrior kings and priests in God's spiritual warfare.

> For we do not wrestle against flesh and blood, but
> against principalities, against powers, against the
> rulers of the darkness of this age, against
> spiritual hosts of wickedness in the heavenly places.
> Ephesians 6:12

God's Got It

Forgiving also allows us the spiritual authority to then define the scope of the relationship, or whether there will be one at all. Forgiveness doesn't automatically mean reconciliation—that takes two.

Soon I learned that once free there was no going back or looking back. Each time I wanted to say something negative about the person who had haunted me, I felt God's peace reassuring me it was going to be okay. I also know that God goes ahead of us and into the midst of our enemies to win our battles. I also know He's on the job when it comes to exacting vengeance for wrongs gone unrighted.

> Avenge not yourselves, beloved, but give place unto the
> wrath of God: for it is written, Vengeance belongeth
> unto me; I will recompense, saith the Lord.
> Romans 12:19

I mean, seriously, who would you rather taking care of those who regale in making others miserable than God himself?

Pillar 4: SERVANTHOOD

> The greatest among you shall be your servant. Whoever
> exalts himself will be humbled, and whoever humbles
> himself will be exalted.
> Matthew 23:11-12

As a rookie patrolman, I was fortunate to have a lieutenant as my commander. Not because of his high position, but because he served as everyone else did. He was the first to respond for help in catching a stray dog, and the last to take credit for a great arrest. I learned so much from this man about servant leadership, even before it became a buzzword on LinkedIn.

While my first lieutenant and others provided great, and some others not so great, examples of being a servant, it is Jesus Christ who we should look to as the example of being a servant.

I think while we love to watch prime-time episodes where a high-powered CEO goes back to work in disguise amongst the galleys, we sometimes fail to understand that Jesus was the first Undercover Boss.

Culturally, we object to the word and idea of being a servant. Its connotation is slave, or indentured servitude. Both obviously a negative in our lexicon, but to drag the word and concept of servant with it is a disservice to the value of having a servant's heart.

Let's give an extra effort to see ourselves not in a position of being done for, but in leading through the example of doing for others.

> For even the Son of Man came not to be served but to
> serve, and to give his life as a ransom for many.
> Mark 10:45

Control

Control is something important for us men. We want it. We hate losing it. Sometimes we resent others for having it. Understanding we have zero control is freedom. Allowing God to have control is faith. Find your freedom through faith and know He is in control. This is true especially in our careers.

Like most of us who want to be successful, we understand the earthly value of title and promotion. But, what I always understood, even as a rookie, was that if you had to tell people you were in charge, then you really weren't in charge.

We all know the guy who arrives early with sleeves already rolled up, and gets to work. He's the guy all of the other guys follow lead on. His servant spirit and actions shine as the example for others.

Exhibiting a Godly work ethic and seeing beyond the person you are serving and into the true nature of God ensures that you do what you do for the love of doing, and not the temporal promise of benefit. Tangible benefits are also gained through volunteering to help others either personally or professionally.

The church my family attends has a congregation of about forty-thousand members. One of the core beliefs is to get members involved to serve the body of Christ. It's one of the most active and vibrant congregations I've ever experienced.

It's actually hard to find a spot to volunteer your time, but there's no lack of trying. These are the characteristics others look for when investing, hiring or partnering. Degrees and pedigrees look nice on the wall, helping hands in service look better on the job.

Freedom

Another hang-up I hear men talk about regarding servanthood is freedom. No, not that they don't love their freedom, but they're afraid they'll lose it. One man I mentored said he was concerned that by surrendering to a servant lifestyle to Christ, that he would lose control and the freedom to do whatever he wanted to do in his own life.

The reality about a servant's life is that by giving it away, we gain more than if we'd held tight. It's like tithing your minimum 10 percent.

God can do more with your 10 percent than you can do with your 100 percent. It's about faith and trust that, in giving away with a sincere heart, God will return the blessing plus some. We never lose when we give.

Serving God isn't a burden on our time. It's an investment in eternal life and a blessing in the natural and spiritual realm. Mediocrity is one of the anchors that tie us down.

Sure, if given a Lamborghini we'd take it, but that's not what defines who we are. We've lost the hard edge to dream and dare to pursue life's blessing on a grand scale. What defines us is not what we drive, but who we serve.

Who will you serve?

> It shall not be so among you. But whoever would be
> great among you must be your servant.
> Matthew 20:26

Pillar 5: COMPASSION

When he went ashore he saw a great crowd, and he had
compassion on them and healed their sick.
Matthew 14:14

Confident alpha males don't strut around bullying people. Have you ever heard of the warrior's whisper? Seldom do you see capable men running a loud mouth. No, in their humble state of ability, they speak with a calm and compassionate tone.

Even in conflict, there is no need to show anything other than the inner spirit-man to an external world. Compassion is a result of the inner spirit-man that shines through as confident, calm and cool under all situations.

Jesus showed us the perfect example of compassion, and while we've spent years wrapping ourselves into a calloused cocoon of testosterone, it's time to Man Up by letting our guard down. Being compassionate reveals a God-nature to ourselves and to others.

How compassionate are you? Do you help old ladies across the street? Do you donate money to charities, or maybe sponsor a child overseas? How about volunteering time and effort for the homeless or elderly? There are many ways to show our compassion and support. Of course, there are lots of opportunities to avoid it.

We get caught up in the rush of the daily grind and might blow past someone in need. Or, maybe it's one of our kids who just doesn't know how to share that they're hurting or simply missing us. It's easy for those we love to get caught up in the wash of life. It doesn't make us uncompassionate, but it does make us inattentive. And that's an easy fix by pulling back on the throttle and making sure our priorities are Godly aligned. Here's a priority checklist for making it easy:

- God
- Wife
- Kids
- Family
- Everything else

While we all have the capacity to show compassion, we don't all exercise that ability. There was nothing that resembled compassion in my childhood home, so when I grew up, it was something that didn't come naturally. Did you catch that? Naturally!

Of course it doesn't come natural because it's an outward expression of a supernatural effect in our lives. I, just like you, learned compassion through Christ, and if we were fortunate, from Christlike examples in our lives. I was even freaked out when others showed compassion to me. It must be modeled to be understood and applied.

Those of us who lagged behind in the compassion department

usually grew up with a "suck-it-up" dad. They are this culture's most common household models, and they force sons to shove emotion deep down inside, for the sake of being tough. This is usually the source of toxic masculinity.

As a result, there are millions of "tough" men skulking through life. They're on the verge of imploding because their life of compressed past pain was never allowed to spiritually manifest. Hurt people hurt people; and unless we've pursued healing from that past, we're prime candidates to repeat the callousness. After all, you only know what you know, right?

Compassion has a root in Latin, and means "co-suffering." It's what made Jesus such an amazing example during His ministry on earth. Jesus actually "felt" people. His sense of others was reflected in His sense of self.

> And Jesus, immediately knowing in himself that virtue
> had gone out of him, turned him about in the press,
> and said, Who touched my clothes? And his disciples
> said unto him, Thou seest the multitude thronging
> thee, and sayest thou, Who touched me? And he
> looked round about to see her that had done this
> thing. But the woman fearing and trembling,
> knowing what was done in her, came and fell down
> before him, and told him all the truth. And he said
> unto her, Daughter, thy faith hath made thee whole;
> go in peace, and be whole of thy plague.
> Mark 25:30-34

Years ago I was standing in church as worship music began, and people were still moving about. Like voices whispering inside my soul, I began looking around the congregation and actually began to "see" the people around me. I saw, and understood what each person was going through. While I wasn't experiencing actual pain, I sensed the pain they were carrying.

I stood in awe, and a calm washed over me. The Holy Spirit moved to tell me that what I was experiencing was compassion. Not just feeling bad for someone else, but actually "feeling" someone else. The sensation of co-suffering with others was an incredibly moving experience. It allowed just a glimpse into the depth of compassion Christ has for us, and oh, what a miraculous glimpse it was.

If you grew up without it, or currently are lacking in compassion, you too can change. The ability to feel for others, including yourself, comes by drawing close to God through prayer. It's an important part of Godly manhood, and don't worry, showing compassion isn't a sign of weakness. It's a motivator for connecting with people who are experiencing physical, emotional or spiritual struggles.

When you reflect God's light to others in need, you shine that blessing back on yourself. Even if you're not the sensitive type, compassion is a rational act when applied to a sense of justice and fair play. Whatever your motivation, being compassionate not only connects your spiritual side to a supernatural understanding of Christ but gives you new opportunities for expanding your capacity to relate to others and better understand yourself. An added bonus is that by exercising compassion, you further develop patience and wisdom.

Who couldn't use more of both?

Pillars of the Better Man

The five pillars we covered are just that. They are foundations to build upon. Each lead to so many more open doors and growth opportunities for improvement. It's like getting buffed up; you can't go one day a month and hope to improve or stay in shape. Bro-building is a daily operation.

I'd mentioned earlier that it takes about thirty days to effect a substantial change in your daily habits. These are only five things that have the supernatural potential for changing your life forever. Make it your goal to pray every day, stick to something (daily prayer!), actively forgiving people who have hurt you, serve others without expectation of reward or even thanks, and work to show compassion.

From one alpha male brother to another, I promise you that life will look very different between the first and the last day. If you're truly brave, then show yourself the courageous warrior who is willing to sacrifice who you are today for who God wants you to become. Travel this journey over one month, and you will never be the same.

8

FUELING YOUR INNER MAN

My home church has an incredible prophetic ministry. My wife and I were selected to participate because we serve as marriage small-group leaders. It was powerful, and as three people spoke prophetic words into my life, this verse was revealed to me through earlier prayer and one of the ministers.

It could be spoken over the life of every man, and would hold value within their life. I wanted to share it with you as you go forward with building the better man.

> Blessed is the man who walks not in the counsel of the
> unGodly, nor stands in the path of sinners, nor sits in
> the seat of the scornful; But his delight is in the law
> of the Lord, and in His law he meditates day and
> night. He shall be like a tree planted by the rivers of
> water, that brings forth its fruit in its season, whose
> leaf also shall not wither; and whatever he does shall
> prosper.
> Psalm 1:1-3

The five pillars we just covered are words that I prayed for and were revealed to me to be shared with you. I want to wrap this building process up with a few more words that are scripturally identified as fruits of the Holy Spirit.

They are gifts because most don't come naturally to us men. Haven't we seen a lot of that? But this is where we build up our spirit-man. The one who does the stuff that doesn't come naturally, and the one who will coach you into a life beyond your wildest imagination.

> But the fruit of the Spirit is love, joy, peace, forbearance, kindness, goodness, faithfulness, gentleness and self-control. Against such things there is no law.
> Galatians 5:22-23

Love

The first of these gifts that I pray over you is love. Did you know that love is not an emotion? Let that sink in while you question having bought candy hearts and flowers. Love is a choice, and in the New Testament, it's called agape love.

I know most of us think about romantic love (eros) when we mention love. Those candies and flowers were bought either for an apology or with memory-making expectations. I know, I'm a man, and have done it too.

Agape love is unconditional, never ending and sacrificial. This is the love I encourage you to show to others. If you currently don't do it, remember, it's a choice, so in your purposeful process of building that better man, you can decide right now to practice agape love.

> A new commandment I give to you, that you love one another: just as I have loved you, you also are to love one another.
> John 13:34

When we show his character through our willingness to be open and vulnerable to others, we not only attract them to us, but gain through the connection of a healthy, loving relationship.

I'm not talking about sexual relationships. I'm talking about the true, intimate connections that God created us to enjoy with Him, and share with each other. Remember, men, loving is a choice. What will you choose?

> We love because he first loved us.
> 1 John 4:19

Joy

The second fruit of the Spirit that I pray over you is joy. Before we focused on building the better man, most of our daily grind was focused on being happy. Maybe it was happiness with a new job, new car, getting in better shape or a great relationship.

These are all fantastic, but they are temporary and depend on external forces. Being happy also requires a constant pursuit of something beyond yourself. The momentary satisfaction always leads to a need for refilling the happy tank.

Joy of the Spirit is eternal and remains a part of who you've become no matter how your life is going. There is no work required to experience the joy of the Lord.

There's an awesome calm in your spirit that leads to your life. Being a Godly man also means you understand the value of helping others who may be struggling as you once were.

> It is a joy for the just to do justice, but destruction will
>   come to the workers of iniquity.
> Proverbs 21:15

Peace

The third fruit of the Spirit that I pray over you is peace. I'm not sure why this word is sometimes a dirty word in a man's life, but once you've constructed the better man, you'll see that it's a valuable asset in your life. Unfortunately, many of us don't know how to handle peace in our life. We see it as boredom, and because there is a restless spirit in our life, we instantly jump into the fray to avoid having the calm that also allows emotions to roam.

> On the evening of that first day of the week, when the
> disciples were together, with the doors locked for
> fear of the Jewish leaders, Jesus came and stood
> among them and said, "Peace be with you!"
> John 20:19

Jesus valued the fruit of peace in His life and those that believed in the good news of the gospel. The Bible highlights three areas of peace that we should also pursue. Personal peace of mind, peace in our relationships, and peace among all nations, peoples and cultures. Spiritual peace is being content in the promises of God, no matter the seasons or storms in life.

Shalom

Patience

The fourth fruit of the Spirit that I pray over you is patience. How patient would you be if everyone you cared about doubted you, and those that hated you constantly planned your demise? How composed would you remain if hassled by crowds of people mocking you while others demanded your time? Sounds a lot like most of our days, doesn't it?

The Greek word for patience is *makrothumia*, and means forbearance or longsuffering. This is akin to our expression of having a long fuse. Patience is also defined as waiting without complaint. I gotta be honest, that's a tall order. But when we look at Jesus, no matter if it was Judas betraying Him or the Pharisees and Sadducees plotting against Him, He always showed patience.

Of course, Jesus wasn't waiting to knock off of work, or until friends called to go to the gym. He waited patiently on His Father. This is the value of practicing patience. Keeping our focus fixed on God whether we're having the time of our life, or questioning a lifetime. Did you notice what I said: "practicing patience."

> Be patient, then, brothers and sisters, until the Lord's coming. See how the farmer waits for the land to yield its valuable crop, patiently waiting for the autumn and spring rains.
> James 5:7

This is why we are to surrender our flesh to the supernatural realm of the Holy Spirit's leading. The gifts are specific and intentional for reflecting the character of God. It's also an exercise in receiving. We're the ones who take charge whether it's wanted or not. But we don't do well when it comes to receiving gifts or help. Again, that's our carnal side of natural-man. Practicing patience is not only wise, it's the gateway to growing closer to God and expanding our spiritual ability to welcomingly receive His gifts and blessings.

So, the key to all of this is…wait for it…patience!

Kindness

The fifth fruit of the Spirit that I pray over you is kindness. In a global study of thirty-seven cultures, people (both men and women) rated kindness as the trait they desired most in a mate. Another study discovered that self-described school bullies bully other kids because they liked the way it made them feel. The takeaway from this is that although people desire to be treated with kindness, being kind doesn't come naturally. It is a supernatural gift of the Spirit, and that is what makes it so desirable.

The Greek word for kind is *chrestos*, and includes the meaning of usefulness in it. The Spirit's fruit of kindness is an action word that includes self-sacrifice and generosity on our part. This action should include speaking words of life over others like I'm doing for you. Show courtesy, giving sincere compliments and even correction are all courageous acts of kindness.

Yes, I said courage. Why? Because any man can glide through daily life without taking the chance to step out beyond himself to help another. It requires courage to step up especially when not asked to show your Godly spirit-man is on duty.

Goodness

The sixth fruit of the Spirit that I pray over you is goodness. God's nature is goodness, and He only acts within His nature. We on the other hand are born into the original sin of Adam and Eve, so goodness doesn't come so natural to us. Of course it doesn't, right? Otherwise, goodness like so many other gifts wouldn't be received as spiritual fruits. I know you see the pattern here because it is by impeccable design.

God wants us to be doing good, and is another action word that also applies to building that better man. Goodness is putting God's nature into practice. Jesus reflected that good nature during His time on earth. He put it into action everywhere He went. Now, not everything was a bed of roses, but even when Jesus had to put the smackdown on people, it was always in a posture of goodness.

> ...how God anointed Jesus of Nazareth with the Holy
> Spirit and power, and how he went around doing
> good and healing all who were under the power of
> the devil, because God was with him.
> Acts 10:38

Faithfulness

The seventh fruit of the Spirit that I pray over you is faithfulness. This is a tough one for us because it requires surrender. Most of us would rather fight than pull out the white flag, but you know that we're not talking about defeat. What we are talking about is having total faith in God's promise so that we are freely willing to surrender all of our natural-man over to the supernatural power of the Holy Spirit.

The spirit of faithfulness will give you a confidence that rises above all circumstances in this life. Not because you won't have to deal with drama, but because no matter what the drama involves, you have the faith that God is always in control, and that He loves you without condition. God will come through!

> For by grace you have been saved through faith, and that
>   not of yourselves; it is the gift of God, not of works,
>   lest anyone should boast.
> Ephesians 2:8-9

Gentleness

The eighth fruit of the Spirit that I pray over you is gentleness. Gentleness isn't a word most of us men would feature in our LinkedIn profile or on our tombstone, yet it's one of the fruits of the Holy Spirit. When you consider the endless list of attributes in human personal behavior, there are only nine that are of the Spirit.

There is a high premium placed upon gentleness, so either we're looking at it the wrong way, or it's time to realign our spirit with what God knows are the most important characteristics. Gentleness is an expression of compassion, seen in God's dealings with the frail and weak, and expected of believers in their dealings with others.

It's like arm wrestling a toddler. Can you crush him in record time? Yeah, sure, but will you? No, never. That, my Brother, is gentleness. Now, the key is to translate that example into our daily life. Expressing the gentleness of Christ in our daily walk shows a blessing from the Holy Spirit, and also reflects God's light upon you and onto others.

Gentleness also does not prohibit us from kicking tail and taking names when the occasion arises. I always think about Jesus cleansing the temple. He showed His ability to rise to the occasion with force, when force was necessary. Men, we can be gentle as lambs, but ferocious as lions. Jesus was no weeping willow.

> Jesus entered the temple courts and drove out all who
> were buying and selling there. He overturned the
> tables of the money changers and the benches of
> those selling doves. "It is written," he said to
> them, "'My house will be called a house of prayer,' but
> you are making it 'a den of robbers.'"
> Matthew 21:12-13

Self-Control

The last fruit of the Spirit that I pray over you is self-control. Before His ministry was launched, Jesus spent time being tempted by the devil in the wilderness. Although He was offered food, power and many other things, Jesus controlled His desires and submitted them all to the will of the Father. Yes, He had desires for food and such, but He had a greater desire to obey God and accomplish what He set out to do.

How many times have we been told, or told others, "You better get ahold of yourself." But what that exactly means depends on where you are in your faith walk. As you build that better man, it means restraint and consideration of others as well as yourself. How are your actions affecting other people, and most importantly, how are they reflecting God's light through you? When you give God control, He returns into you the fruit of self-control.

A man without self-control is like a city broken into and
left without walls.
Proverbs 25:28

9

BEING THE GOD MADE MAN

Brother, it doesn't matter if you're a titan of industry, all-galaxy athlete, still living in your folks' basement or just trying to get by, God has a plan for you. It might mean talking in front of millions of people, or it might be fighting to save your marriage. All that matters is you are here on this earth today for a reason.

Some of you may know that reason, while others may pursue it for a lifetime only to discover that pursuit was your purpose. We are all unique and wonderfully made, so to each his own path as long as we all meet back up where it all began—with God.

There are so many issues we can talk about as men, and every single one of them is valid. We are in a tough spot today, but now you see that it wasn't something only you did. We have a history of messing things up, but that doesn't mean we have to expect a future of doing the same things wrong over and over again.

It also means that if you make the decision at this very moment to stop the string of errors that have plagued you, then you and your kids (or future kids) and every generation of yours to come will know victory instead of the shame, pain and guilt that you may have struggled with up until today.

When we think of leaving a family legacy it always comes in the image of stacks of cash, cars and material goods. The truth is, we aren't Richie Rich, and most of us simply worry about paying the monthly mortgage. The grand ideal of leaving a legacy signals that we are failures because there is no pot of gold to proudly hand down to our spawn.

Money isn't your measure of worth. But on a side note, does God want to bless us, even financially? Yes indeed!! But He must trust you before He can bless you.

God will only give to you once He knows He can give through you. How do you gain that trust? Manning Up through these scriptural principles will go a long way toward drawing super close in your walk with Him. Remember:

"Trust is built in drops, and lost in buckets."

—*Pastor Jimmy Evans*

So back to you leaving a family legacy, please don't equate your future value to the generations to come with what money you leave. The greatest investment you will make in the future of your family is to share God's Word with them. The best way to share it is to show it. Most Bible lessons are caught, not taught.

Build that better man, and I promise you the world will notice. How can you have the light of Christ shining through you and it not explode like a beacon on a hill?

I know some men prefer not to draw the added attention, but even if it's just you and your kid over weekend visitation, they will see God in you and through you. Trust me, that will pay more dividends in your child's future than a hundred-dollar bill in their pocket.

Look, I know it's tough to change course. I used to lead my family by being the boss. That meant my word was the law, and although I never even considered being forceful, by sheer presence, I dominated my family.

Guess who used to do the same thing to dominate his family? Yep, my dad. I wanted to become a better man and thus a Godly dad, but on my own, I had no idea how. So I got frustrated, and defaulted to what I knew—being in command.

Now don't get me wrong. I am the spiritual head of my family, but that's not the same thing as acting like a job site foreman. Building that better man through God's Word and example showed me in very practical terms how to change course.

It also applies to people outside of your immediate family. There's a phrase, "Who's in your five?", that is useful for men. Socially, you are the aggregate of the five people closest to you.

I like to say, "Show me your friends and I'll show you your future." You want to know another truth? Most men don't even have five close friends. The national average is between zero and one. That's heartbreaking because it's true.

Take an honest look at your life. I'm not talking about your work buddies or that dude at the gym you nod to when you're both by the arm curl machine.

I'm talking about friends. You've been to their house, they hung out while you confessed sadness over a lost relationship, they drove across country for your parent's funeral or your child's birth.

Separating mere acquaintances from true friends, how many do you have? When I left law enforcement and relocated to Dallas, Texas, I realized that I had exactly zero friends.

Sure, I had hundreds of acquaintances, and maybe thousands of people in my circle of influence, but once I walked away from behind that thin blue line, the truth was, I was all alone.

Why do we find ourselves isolated in such a crowded world? Because we do not naturally possess the fruits of the Spirit. These are the qualities that other people look for in friends.

If we were in a fortified compound hunting violent felons, then all I want are the toughest, battle-tested warriors. But the reality in life is that we aren't in those hostile environments often if at all. Yet this is the hard exterior we portray, and yet we wonder why we're alone at the end of the day.

Once I built that better man, I dropped the protective shield, and I began to pursue friendships with other men. It was weird at first. I worried that they'd get the wrong impression, so I played it cool, but the truth was, most of my now-Brothers were as alone as I was.

The more I relied on the very same biblical principles I share with you in God Made Man, the more blessed my life as a remodeled alpha man became.

Brother, I'm not trying to sell you on anything other than yourself. You are the product and the prize. You've allowed it to sit on the back of the shelf collecting dust while the rewards of a blessed life have passed you by.

It's not too late. The time is now. I'm helping you understand how to best knock off that dust, sharpen your focus, and get back in the game of living a conqueror's life in Christ.

I am praying for you. We might not have met in person yet, but one day, be it here or up top, I know we're going to have a great time hanging out together.

I want to hear all about what God did for you, and in return what you set out to do for Him. There's so much work waiting for us, and so many men who need to hear His good Word.

Sometimes it's hard to bring up these topics with another man. It's hard to talk about them with your own kids. I know it was for me, and that's when God led me to write this book.

Whether you invest in one or all of them, I do pray that you know what you've read is only what God led me to share. Honestly, a lot of the personal stuff was hard to write, but God knew as much as you needed to see it, that I needed to share it.

Building that better man goes a long way in helping ourselves and other Brothers in this life. Sure, we can walk by someone laid flat on their back, but that's only continuing to walk in the darkness of what drove us to search for light in the first place.

Being that better man is reaching out to give of ourselves even when it would be easier to just look the other way. Trust me, you will always get back more from giving than you can ever give away.

So, at the very start of this journey I made a promise to you. That promise was not to bore you, and because you've read through the entire thing, I'm going to assume it wasn't boring. Thanks again for investing your time into your life.

I also wanted to start a conversation about embracing your alpha manhood without having to worry about being attacked for it. The key to this conversation is redefining what an alpha male is. We've based everything on God's example of manhood.

Whether you're a believer or not, these truths are as much about blue-collar common-sense principles as they are about being spiritually inspired. The key is that you choose what parts of God Made Man speak power into your life and you claim them as your own.

Finally, there are other books in the series that drill down into very specific topics that trouble and challenge us men. You've begun laying the foundation with this book, so I encourage you to look at the other topics that might help strengthen you in your daily walk. Remember, this isn't about scraping by in the shadows, this is strutting chin up in the LIGHT.

God bless you, Brother,
Scott

DISCUSSION GUIDE

Brothers,

You're here! Thanks again for making this investment into your own life. Your efforts today will pay off big time for your family and friends in the time to come.

These lessons are designed not as a test or final exam (man, I hated taking tests in school) but as a way for you to go back over what it was that you've read.

The best way for men to take information and apply it to our daily lives is by going back over it in a practical manner by giving examples.

Each lesson has questions about the connected chapter. These questions are about you, not about what I wrote. This is your personal journal, so please don't hold back on the answers because you're afraid of what someone might think. This is for you.

This is the right time to Man Up because it's your time to claim the blessed life that God has created for you. You are the man!

Welcome to Manhood God's way,
Scott

DISCUSSION GUIDE: LESSON 1

THIS WEEK'S DISCUSSION QUESTIONS ARE BASED ON CHAPTER 1.

KEY VERSE:

And if one prevail against him, two shall withstand him; and a threefold cord is not quickly broken.
Ecclesiastes 4:12

KEY THOUGHT:

There is so much more to this life than wondering what it's about. It doesn't matter whether you live in a mansion or a tent, living a life outside of God's grace is not living at all. We've been sold a false bill of goods, and until we're ready to stop running to nowhere inside of the hamster wheel, we will never fully enjoy the measure of peace and blessings that God has ordained in our life. Let's claim that victory through Christ!

DISCUSSION QUESTIONS:

1. How do you define what it is to be a man?

2. Is there a difference between being a man and being a Godly man? If so, describe.

3. Write out a few consequences you have suffered as a result of poor life choices.

4. What is your relationship with God? Go deeper in your description than saying whether you believe in Him or not.

5. Give this an honest attempt, but are you ready and willing to build the better man? Why or why not?

APPLICATION QUESTION:

Have you tried being a better you? If so, what happened either right or wrong, and why are you at the point of wanting to give it another go?

DISCUSSION GUIDE: LESSON 2

THIS WEEK'S DISCUSSION QUESTIONS ARE BASED ON CHAPTER 2.

KEY VERSE:

Behold, I stand at the door, and knock: if any man hear my voice, and open the door, I will come in to him, and will sup with him, and he with me.
   Revelation 3:20

KEY THOUGHT:

I'm not sure if you realized that God Made Man was based on God's Word, but it is the instruction manual for life. It's also the best medicine for healing from what has hurt you. There really is no way to avoid this, so if you're truly wanting to change your life and willing to trust me for a bit, I promise you won't get drained over religion. All I'll share is truth and hope. Deal?

DISCUSSION QUESTIONS:

1. What is free will in terms of God's relation to us?

2. Do you focus on living life with purpose? In everything you say and do, is there a purpose to or for it? Why or why not?

3. Talking about submission in life, how do you see it as it relates to you, and do you feel that you are able to submit to an authority over your life?

4. What steps have you taken to purposefully improve your life?

5. What steps are you not willing to take, even if it meant improving your life?

6. Exactly what improvements do you want out of life?

APPLICATION QUESTION:

I've tried diets where they give you a list of foods you can eat. Despite what was proven to work, almost every time I decided what I would and wouldn't eat, I failed to lose weight. Are you committed to building the better you, and if so, will you dedicate this season of your life to making that change? Why or why not?

DISCUSSION GUIDE: LESSON 3

THIS WEEK'S DISCUSSION QUESTIONS ARE BASED ON CHAPTER 3.

KEY VERSE:

Honor your father and your mother: that your days may be long on the land which the Lord your God gives you.
Exodus 20:12

KEY THOUGHT:

We learn about God from our earthly dads, so if you had a poor relationship with yours, or none at all, then you may be working from a deficit in your foundation for faith. If that is the case, please don't let that throw you. God is our ultimate Father and although we may not have known it, He's always loved us.

DISCUSSION QUESTIONS:

1. What was your faith experience as a child and young adult?

1. Describe your relationship with your dad. Are there things you must forgive him for? If so, now's the time to begin working to forgive.
2. When did you first start thinking about God, and how did you first come to hear about Him?
3. What is your personal identity tied to? Is it work, awards, money, etc.?
4. Write out in detail what your priorities are in life.

APPLICATION QUESTION:

A big part of this section is identifying who you are and what affects from your past influenced that man. We accumulate spiritual connections to past people and events that caused us pain or still disturbs us even today. These require forgiving those who hurt us before we can move forward. Big question—are you willing to free yourself from that past by forgiving everyone who hurt you?

DISCUSSION GUIDE: LESSON 4

THIS WEEK'S DISCUSSION QUESTIONS ARE BASED ON CHAPTER 4.

KEY VERSE:

Watch, stand fast in the faith, be brave, be strong. Let all that you do be done with love.
  1 Corinthians 16:13-14

KEY THOUGHT:

Mission focused is where we excel. When it comes to the charge to Man Up, we will fail to accomplish the mission without clear instructions. They are not meant to imply that we cannot navigate our way, but the action items are meant to keep us focused and on the fast track to success. Allow this section to speak to you, and focus on how you may best accomplish each mission objective.

DISCUSSION QUESTIONS:

1. Describe the differences between Man Up from a Christian versus a non-Christian perspective.

2. Write out what 1 Corinthians 16:13-14 speaks to you and how you can apply it to your life.

3. Write out in detail a list of sins from which you have yet to repent. Most of us carry guilt over sin, but feeling guilty doesn't bring about repentance and restoration – conviction brings repentance. So take the time to focus on answering this question.

4. What does the idea of being a servant speak to you? Explain your answer in terms how practicing service to others might affect your life.

5. Think through each of the action items. Which do you practice regularly? Regarding the ones you don't practice, describe how you will begin to apply them to your life.

APPLICATION QUESTION:

We're almost half way into our mission to build the better man. It's time to assess where you are. You should have grown "roots" by this point by having committed to each task and praying over the content as it applies to your life. If you're still struggling to press the bar overhead, no worries, but please take this time to consider what it is that might be holding you back.

DISCUSSION GUIDE: LESSON 5

THIS WEEK'S DISCUSSION QUESTIONS ARE BASED ON CHAPTER 5.

KEY VERSES:

Do not be misled: "Bad company corrupts good character."
1 Corinthians 15:33 (NIV)

KEY THOUGHT:

We are at war, and whether you know it or even care to accept it, this is real. Recall what is said in 1 Peter 5:8 about satan prowling like a lion looking to devour you. Of course, this is no reason to be afraid unless you are living outside the will of God.

But we men have been under serious attack of late for nothing more than being men. We are living in precarious times, and while I'm not trying to sound the alarms, it is time to take stock of what's going down around you.

DISCUSSION QUESTIONS:

1. God designed us for relationships. How do you approach your relationships? Are your friends dear to your heart, or mostly buds you call to hang out with on occasion? List out the names of your closest friends, and describe what role they play in your life.

2. If you have or would serve as a mentor for another man, describe what it is you have to offer that relationship?

3. Write out your opinion of where we are as men in the grand scheme of today's world.

4. Do you feel as though you have influence in the world, your family, your circle of peers, or just in your own life? Describe why or why not and what you can do to purposefully change the situation.

5. Do you act intentionally throughout the day, or do you just go with the flow? Do you feel like you are connected to others through meaningful relationships? How about with God?

APPLICATION QUESTION:

Are you where you want to be in life? Is this what you imagined your life would be like? If not, describe what the conflicts are and where you could've chosen differently to have effected different results. Big question; do you have a teachable spirit that is open to correction, redemption and change?

DISCUSSION GUIDE: LESSON 6

THIS WEEK'S DISCUSSION QUESTIONS ARE BASED ON CHAPTER 6.

KEY VERSE:

For by grace you have been saved through faith, and that not of yourselves; it is the gift of God, not of works, lest anyone should boast.
Ephesians 2:8-9

KEY THOUGHT:

You are not in this alone!

God is so crazy about us, yet we resist Him because we think it's giving up our freedom, or that He'll know about our sins. Guess what? He already knows about the darkness in your life, so why not come into the light where His grace may bless you? If you are constantly getting knocked around by life, then it's your own stubbornness that keeps you there. The choice is yours, but God is really hoping you'll choose wisely.

DISCUSSION QUESTIONS:

1. Do you believe we men are doing much better than Adam did? Explain why or why not?

2. Understanding that we all have sinned and fall short (way short) of God's glory, do you have shame over your sins or over refusing to not confess them for forgiveness by God?

3. Better question is; do you honestly believe that God will instantly forgive you, or are you afraid that He will punish you?

4. Write out a list of what you consider to be your worst sins. Describe what it is that causes you to commit them, attempts in the past to stop committing them, and how you feel every time you commit them.

5. Do you believe that you can have eternal life with God if all you do is have faith in His son, Jesus Christ? Are you comfortable with that truth, or do you feel like you have to work to prove your belief? Explain why, and also what you could do to impress God so much that He'd ignore His Son, Jesus?

APPLICATION QUESTION:

Too many of us are suspicious by nature. Someone does something kind for us, and we ask what's the catch. There is nothing more kind or giving than what God gave to us in the form of His only Son, Jesus Christ. His gift is so that we can keep a relationship with God. Maybe God should've kept a bunch of rules attached so that we'd have to work like dogs to earn our way into heaven. But He mercifully did not do that because He loves us. Do you believe this, and are you willing to accept God's free gift of salvation?

DISCUSSION GUIDE: LESSON 7

THIS WEEK'S DISCUSSION QUESTIONS ARE BASED ON CHAPTER 7.

KEY VERSES:

One day Jesus was praying in a certain place. When he finished, one of his disciples said to him, "Lord, teach us to pray, just as John taught his disciples."

Luke 11:1

KEY THOUGHT:

We have choices in this life, and the key to living a blessed life through building the better man is in deciding wisely. There is a constant struggle between our natural man and our spirit man. The truth is, they were designed to live in harmony for the sake of creating the best man possible. Let's focus on finding that balance and you will immediately see the benefits of living a full life.

DISCUSSION QUESTIONS:

1. Walking through each of the 5 pillars—Do you pray daily? How about constantly? Describe your prayer life and how has it benefited you. How can you improve it to improve you?

2. Walking through each of the 5 pillars—Are you a man of your word? Commitment matters, so describe what it means to you, how have you shown it and what are the consequences of breaking yours?

3. Walking through each of the 5 pillars—Have you forgiven everyone who has hurt you? Understanding that unless you forgive others, God will not forgive you, who do you need to forgive right now?

4. Walking through each of the 5 pillars—Do you find joy in serving others? Servanthood is sacrificial love and best illustrated by Christ. Describe areas of service where you enjoy placing others above yourself, and also ways that you can become more involved in serving others.

5. Walking through each of the 5 pillars—Do you show compassion to others, or even to yourself? Most men aren't naturally compassionate, but through prayer and gifting of the Holy Spirit, we may come to know the fruits of a compassionate spirit. Describe what showing compassion means to you. How might you put compassion into practical application?

APPLICATION QUESTION:

The 5 Pillars for building a better man are individual in nature, but vital in the holistic approach toward being a better you. It's easy to focus on one or two while neglecting the rest. It's even easier to come up with your own list, but if you are serious about making this time the right time for living a blessed life, are you willing to apply each of these 5 foundational practices to daily living?

DISCUSSION GUIDE: LESSON 8

THIS WEEK'S DISCUSSION QUESTIONS ARE BASED ON CHAPTER 8.

KEY VERSE:

But the fruit of the Spirit is love, joy, peace, forbearance, kindness, goodness, faithfulness, gentleness and self-control. Against such things there is no law.

Galatians 5:22-23

KEY THOUGHT:

Understanding that we are like a rubber tire without air helps us comprehend the role of the Holy Spirit in our lives. Can that heap of deflated rubber be useful? Sure, maybe as a doorstop or something, but without the filling of air (the Holy Spirit), that tire will never realize its full potential.

It has an incredible life designed to travel wonderful roads and deliver so many adventures to the rubber tire properly filled. This is our connection with the Holy Spirit. God sent Him to live with and within us so that God Himself would remain with us. The Spirit is God's gift.

DISCUSSION QUESTIONS:

1. Take an honest personal assessment. Do you feel that you naturally possess any or all of the fruits of the Spirit? If so, which ones? Describe in what ways do you exhibit each?

2. Do you think your life would be better off having the ability to exhibit each of the fruits of the Spirit? If so, describe how each improves your life and the interaction with others.

3. Describe your understanding of a triune God (the Trinity,) and how each one (Father, Son & Holy Spirit) serve, guide and benefit your life.

4. Which of the fruits of the Spirit are you more inclined to exercise, and why?

5. Which of the fruits of the Spirit are you less attracted to? Does it present an issue or a roadblock? How can you overcome this barrier?

APPLICATION QUESTION:

Each of these gifts of the Holy Spirit are designed to be exercised first through your spirit-man so that they may be shown externally by your natural man. Because they are from the Spirit, we don't usually just walk around with an abundance of each or all. Will you commit to starting each day for one week by praying for these gifts?

DISCUSSION GUIDE: LESSON 9

THIS WEEK'S DISCUSSION QUESTIONS ARE BASED ON CHAPTER 9.

KEY VERSE:

He has shown you, O man, what is good; And what does the Lord require of you. But to do justly, To love mercy, And to walk humbly with your God? Micah 6:8 (NKJV)

KEY THOUGHT:

I've been straight with you, and yes, there were times when I knew how tough things would be going in that I hesitated moving forward. I wish I could say that in fact, I always charged ahead, but that would be a lie. But in those times when I felt the most dread is when I gave it all away to God. In fact, those are the times during the worst of times, that I did indeed move forward as I followed safely behind Him.

Manhood is tough. We think we're doing right, but still mess up. The key in the good times and the bad is relationship. Centering our life on a solid, loving and honest relationship with God will ensure that everything else in this life comes in stride and that we will not be overcome by the enemy. That war has already been won, and God is anxious for us to proclaim that victory in our life. Life is for the living —Are you ready to start living life?

DISCUSSION QUESTIONS:

1. Write out in detail what you want your legacy to your family to look like.

2. Develop a purposeful and practical strategy for accomplishing the vision of your family legacy. Include short- and long-term goals.

3. List names and contact information for people with whom you can share this legacy strategy. Include whether they will help you shape your vision, improve your goals, provide guidance for accomplishing the tasks, and will they help hold you accountable.

4. Will you take time to consider what friends you have surrounded yourself with? I believe that if you show me your friends, that I'll show you your future. List your five closest friends (not family, work acquaintances, or old school buds) and describe what each of them bring to your life – good and bad.

5. Describe what you want your life to look like in one year from now. List the types of friends who can help you accomplish this goal. If your current friends do possess the qualities to help you become that better man, then begin to connect with men who do. Eventually, you will find that your current friends that tie you to the past will have to be moved out of your inner circle. Are you willing to make those adjustments so that your closest friends are those who best support your future you?

APPLICATION QUESTION:

What does the best version of you look like? Don't be embarrassed to claim the blessings God has waiting for you to claim. Don't hold back in writing out exactly what you want your life to look like in the very near future. Tip: Start with asking God!!!

DR. SCOTT SILVERII

Dr. Scott Silverii is a son of the Living God. Thankful for the gift of his wife, Leah, they share seven kids, a French bulldog named Bacon and a micro-mini Goldendoodle named Biscuit.

A highly decorated, twenty-five-year law enforcement career promptly ended in retirement when God called Scott out of public service and into HIS service. The "Chief" admits that leading people to Christ is more exciting than the twelve years he spent undercover, sixteen years in SWAT, and five years as chief of police combined.

Scott has earned post-doctoral hours in a Doctor of Ministry degree in addition to a Master of Public Administration and a Ph.D. in Cultural Anthropology. Education and experience allow for a deeper understanding in ministering to the wounded, as he worked to break free from his own past pain and abuse.

In 2016, Scott was led to plant a church. Exclusive to online ministry, Five Stones Church.Online was born out of the calling to combat the negative influences reigning over social media. Scott's alpha manhood model for heroes is defined by, "Be on your guard; stand firm in the faith; be courageous; be strong. Do everything in love." (1 Corinthians 16:13-14)

ALSO BY DR. SCOTT SILVERII

PAY IT FORWARD

- Watch your other Bros 6!
- Share God Made Man with other men.
- Leave a review online wherever you bought this book.
- Post the book and buy links on your social media so others find the help they need.
- Message me for interviews, speaking, blog tour or questions. Personal email - scottsilverii@gmail.com
- Be the Man God created you to be!

ACKNOWLEDGMENTS

I give all glory and praise to my heavenly Father. It was His son, Jesus Christ who lifted me up when I wanted to stay down, and the Holy Spirit who now pours life into my soul so that I may pour out into others.

I want to thank my loving *ezer*, Leah and our wonderfully blended family of kids and a French Bulldog, Bacon.

A special appreciation to my editor, Imogen Howson, and cover artist Darlene Albert of Wicked Smart Design.

More titles from
Five Stones Press

fivestonespress.org